"I was fortunate to meet 'Aunt' Marlene when I was 13 years old. Her vibrant life of faith, sense of adventure, and zeal for following Jesus impacted my life beyond description. Marlene and her late husband, Don, laid a foundation of unswerving faith and commitment to The City Church, now Churchome. Their example of faith—taking God at His Word by walking out their faith in Word and deed—set a high standard for our community as well as thousands of believing communities around the world. Churchome would not be what it is today without their nearly 30-years of dedication.

Marlene has a sparkling personality, is fun and humorous, and an amazing preacher of the Word who takes great pleasure in seeing others succeed by finding their full life in Jesus. May her story of following Him inspire you to do the same!"

Judah & Chelsea Smith
Lead Pastors, Churchome, Kirkland, WA

"In this book, Marlene shares some insightful and powerful principles, plus heartfelt stories, that will inspire you to be more and do more."

Dr. Bob Harrison
Founder, Christian Business Leaders.

"It's one thing to understand the theory of living an exceptional life for God, full of faith, generosity, and big thinking. It's another thing altogether to live out this kind of life.

Marlene has to be one of the most inspiring and faith-filled individuals I've ever met. Her life and her legacy were built on the principles outlined in this incredible book. Marlene, thank you for being someone who God could trust to change the world!"

Drew Davies
Pastor, Hope Village Church, Kirkland, WA

"I've had the pleasure of meeting many faithful and influential people in my life, but Marlene Ostrom is one of the MOST faithful and MOST influential. Her testimony of faith, her resilience, and her heart to love and lead is an example all Christians need to know and follow.

Reading through the pages of this book, I found myself challenged by her faith, humbled by her obedience, and inspired by her impact. In her own humble and gentle way, Marlene tells a story that reminds us that God is at work in our lives and that the miracles she testifies to can be present in our lives as well. This book is one you'll enjoy, be encouraged by, and want to share with others."

Lyle Wells
President, Integrus Leadership

"I've been following Jesus for a long time, but reading Marlene's book has taught me so much about active and expectant faith. She's even gotten me praying out loud as I drive around in my car!"

Josh Kelley
Author, "Radically Normal: You Don't Have to Live Crazy to Follow Jesus"

"Marlene Ostrom's fabulous and life-changing book Making Faith Great Again comes at the perfect time! Her stories and inspiring faith-journey will captivate you and show you how to live a life with no regrets as you follow God's love and purpose.

No matter where you are with God, each of Marlene's chapters will meet you and guide you to greater faith!"

Steve Gutlzer
Author, Speaker, and President of Leadership Quest

MAKING
FAITH
GREAT
AGAIN

*Wisdom from a Life with
No Regrets*

MARLENE OSTROM

MAKING FAITH GREAT AGAIN:
Wisdom from a Life with No Regrets

Copyright ©2020, Marlene Ostrom

Hardcover ISBN: 978-1-7349756-1-1
Paperback ISBN   978-1-954024-02-1

Requests for information should be addressed to:
Mike Acker, 113 Cherry St #35754, Seattle WA 98104

https://www.advantage-publishing.com
To contact, please e-mail: contact@advantage-publishing.com

DEDICATION

I would like to dedicate this book to my four sons Daniel, Doug, Larry and Paul—who stood by me through the trial of losing their father, through years of business and traveling to foreign countries, who are always here when I need them—for their sense of humor during tough situations, and also to their wives—Kim, Cindy, Laine, and Stephanie—who are all inspirations to me.

FORWARD BY
JOHN BEVERE

———— ༄ ————

The life of faith truly is an adventure. In many ways, that's what makes the journey of faith so great—the thrill of the unknown, the certain uncertainty, the laying hold of tomorrow, one day at a time. When you choose to fully follow God, you're consenting to the fact that you will be a pilgrim, abandoning the comfort of being a settler.

Marlene has been a dear friend of mine and Lisa's for many years. We've witnessed her and her late husband, Don, walk out their faith through many highs and lows, tests and trials, miracles and mishaps—all the while retaining a childlike sense of adventure. If I'm honest, I'm concerned we've lost that type of childlike faith in the Western Church. It's possible we've been sedated by the pleasures and pressures of the day-to-day and have succumbed to merely existing rather than truly living.

Two and a half years ago, I sat with Marlene as she was grieving the loss of her husband. In the midst of her heartache, I perceived it was a pivotal moment for her life's purpose. Being a woman of profound wisdom, I encouraged her to start putting pen to paper as I could tell that she had a message brewing within her, and it was only a matter of time before it came forth.

Now is that time!

The message contained in this book, combined with the many personal stories of a life well lived, will ignite your faith and shoot adrenaline into your soul so you, too, can embark on your own adventure with God. More than ever, faith needs to become great again!

Sincerely,

- **John Bevere**
Best-selling Author and Minister, Co-founder of
Messenger International

Contents

CHAPTER 1

The Adventure of Faith

────────── ୬୧୬ ──────────

How would you feel if your husband of two years suddenly asked you to move halfway around the world to live on faith and be a missionary for the rest of your lives? What if you were holding your one-year old son at the time?

It was 1957. Donald was twenty-seven and I was only twenty. For the past two years, he'd pastored a small church in rural Western Washington. We lived in a small home attached to the back of the church. The salary was low and we never had enough money, but those were such happy days! During this occasion, Donald and I were at a mission's conference, listening to a missionary who'd given the past thirty-five years of his life in the Philippines. Without warning, Donald turned to me and said, "God asked if I was willing to give my life in the Philippines. I said yes!"

Imagine what he was asking of me! Leave our families, literally give up everything, and take our son halfway across the world with literally no money. So, what did I say?

"Sounds like an adventure! Yes!"

We didn't know anyone in the Philippines, we didn't have any money, and we didn't know how to speak the language, but we immediately set a date and told our families that we'd be leaving.

The life of faith is an adventure. It doesn't always lead us to easy paths, but it's always an adventure! In Mark 4:35-41, Jesus wanted to go with His disciples to the other side of the Sea of Galilee, so He said to them, "Let us go to the other side!" He was telling them their future—they would arrive safely. So, they all got into the boat and Jesus went to sleep.

> And a furious storm of wind [of hurricane proportions] arose, and the waves kept beating into the boat, so that it was already becoming filled. But He [Himself] was in the stern [of the boat], asleep on the [leather] cushion; and they awoke Him and said to Him, Master, do You not care that we are perishing? And He arose and rebuked the wind and said to the sea, Hush now! Be still (muzzled)! And the wind ceased (sank to rest as if exhausted by its beating) and

there was [immediately] a great calm (a perfect peacefulness).

He said to them, "Why are you so timid and fearful? How is it that you have no faith (no firmly relying trust)?" (AMPC, Mark 4:37-40).

Jesus had declared that they would reach the other side, but when the storm came up and the waves started beating against the sides of their rickety boat, their fear rose up and they forgot all about His words. That's what happens to us. Life's storms start buffeting us and we forget God's promises. So how can we get the faith we need to get to the other side? Romans 10:17 tells us, "faith comes by hearing the Word of God." How can we expect to have faith if we don't read God's Word?

Living by faith requires knowing the Bible and speaking God's promises. We can't claim His promises if we don't even know them! In my "faith adventures," I've learned to not only read His Word for my circumstances but to also speak it out loud! This is so important—speak His Word out loud!

Pay attention to what Jesus said in Mark 11:23-24:

I assure you and most solemnly *say* to you, whoever *says* to this mountain, 'Be lifted up and thrown into the sea!' and does not doubt in his heart [in God's unlimited power], but believes that what he *says* is going to take place, it will be done for him.... For this reason I am telling you, whatever things you ask for in prayer [in accordance with God's will], *believe* [with confident trust] that you have received them, and they will be given to you" (AMP, emphasis added).

Did you notice that he said "say" three times and "believe" only once?

Faith PowerPoint: Don't just pray in your heart, speak God's Word out loud!

It's in the middle of the storm that we will learn to repeat His Word and hold onto it with complete faith: "I will never [under any circumstances] desert you [nor give you up nor leave you without support, nor will I in any degree leave you helpless], nor will I forsake or let you down or relax My hold on you [assuredly not]!" (AMPC, Hebrew 13:5).

Unfortunately, we just don't hear as much about living a life of faith in the church these days. We've lost the eager expectation and dependence on God's miraculous power. But I believe that faith is the foundation of victorious living and successful ministry, business, marriage, parenting, and relationships. I wrote this book to showcase how Donald and I lived a regret-free life by faith. It is my hope and prayer that, together, we can make faith great again!

My father, Carlos Horton, was a man of faith, compassion, generosity, and an adventurous spirit. Adventure runs in my family! His father was a literal pioneer of Nebraska and served as their state legislature. Once, when I was about twelve, Dad loaded me, my mom, and my fourteen-year-old sister Norma Jean, into our 1956 powder blue Ford Fairlane. He drove us from our home in Nebraska all the way to California for a vacation. There were no interstates back then, no cell phones, and no seat belts, so it really was an adventure! I don't remember too much about the trip, other than fighting with Norma Jean in the back seat the whole time.

It didn't matter much where we went. My dad loved to travel and I loved traveling with him. By the time I was sixteen, I'd already seen every state west of the Mississippi. God was preparing me to go to the Philippines long before I even met my Donald!

As I have mentioned, my grandfather was a pioneer and my dad also had that pioneering spirit. He worked in the rest home business (we call them "skilled nursing facilities" now). I grew up watching my dad run these facilities, visiting him at work, and talking to the residents with him—he loved his residents and always treated them like family. Every now and again, he'd say, "I feel called to such and such place," and we'd move to a new town. By the time I was in 8th grade, I'd gone to six different schools. But I didn't mind; to me, it just meant I'd make more friends!

Whenever we came to a new town, Dad would always look for two properties to buy: an old mansion to convert into a nursing home and a piece of property for a new church. He'd put up a temporary church building, bring in traveling evangelists, and find a pastor. Dad didn't preach, but he loved to play the Hawaiian electric guitar (they're called "lap steel guitars" now). He was an excellent player—he used to play with Sol Hoʻopiʻi, who was known as the "King of the Hawaiian Guitar." Anyway, Dad would play the Hawaiian guitar and my sister or I would play the piano. That's how we would get the church meetings started.

In every new town we moved to, my father started a new nursing home and a new church. Churches that he built and funded through his business can still be found throughout the Midwest. I learned, from an early age, that business and ministry should go hand-in-hand, but I had no idea how closely I'd follow in his footsteps! But I'm getting ahead of myself...

When I was sixteen, Dad heard about a facility for sale in Bremerton, Washington (about an hour west of Seattle). Always looking for the next adventure, he packed us up and moved us halfway across the country to Seattle. He bought a really nice house right on Lake Washington. It was very different from Nebraska! Evergreen trees covered the hills on the other side of the lake and Mount Rainier towered unbelievably high over the city (little did I know that I'd be living in its shadow two years later). And, of course, it rained a lot more than it did in Nebraska, but I didn't care. It was just a new adventure!

My sister started attending Northwest Bible College in Seattle—it's since moved to Kirkland and became Northwest University. Between the two of us, Norma Jean (or Jeannie, as everyone but me called her) always seemed to be the more spiritual one. She'd stay up every night saying her prayers and I'd just hop in bed! All she wanted to do with her life was to serve God and help our father. She had such a sensitive and kind heart. Even now, those who remember her speak of her sensitive heart. Norma Jean ended up graduating from the University of Washington as a registered nurse. Even though we were so different, we got along really well and she was so dear to me.

I attended Roosevelt High School (that school is still there and it's pretty well-known in Seattle! Many musicians and politicians got their start there and even two Nobel prize winners). Norma Jean and I would take the city bus together and ride it all the way to Roosevelt, then she'd take it the rest of the way to Northwest. I enjoyed high school and was a really good student—all

A's and B's,—but frequently got sidetracked. I'd start giggling with my friends and the teacher would have to call me out. My parents wanted me to be a lawyer, just like my grandfather, because I had a sharp mind. But then I met Donald.

Here's how we got together. Norma Jean started dating a student at Northwest and I'd go to the college to visit her—but also to get to know John's roommate a little better. So what if I was sixteen and Donald was twenty-three? I just loved his personality. He could walk into a room and make everyone feel at ease. No wonder he was the student body president. He was always joking and having fun; just like me. We hit it off so well. And he was so handsome! But more than anything, he had a heart for God. From the very beginning, I knew that he loved God and wanted to serve Him with his whole life. That was so important to me.

We started dating and were engaged by the time I was seventeen. Because I was so young, a lot of people criticized us, but my parents liked him and were fine with it. Anyway, Donald graduated from college and I graduated from high school. He was hired as an Associate Pastor at Broadway Tabernacle in Seattle. This is when Dr. Derek Prince was still an evangelist there.

Now Donald was also raised in a strong Christian home and attended an Assemblies of God church. They were very poor and he remembered having to skin rabbits for their dinner. In those days, a lot of Christians believed you couldn't be rich and be close to God. They were taught that money was the root of all evil. But that isn't what God's Word teaches: "For the *love of money* [that is, the greedy desire for it and the willingness to gain it unethically] is a root of all sorts of evil..." (AMPC, 1 Timothy 6:10, emphasis added). Once, when he was a teenager, he saw a man drive a shiny new Cadillac to church and wondered, "What is *he* doing at church?" God had a lot to teach him!

From the beginning, Donald and I decided we didn't want to depend on my parents or their money. He even turned down my father's offer to join the family business because we knew God had called us into ministry. We had a nice, but simple, wedding at Broadway Tabernacle. There certainly wasn't dancing or anything like that. I don't think I even wore any make up—Christians were pretty strict back then! We'd saved up our money for a little three-day honeymoon in Northern California. We couldn't be away for any longer than that because Donald had been hired as the pastor at a little church in Mineral, Washington. He was scheduled to start two weeks after our wedding. We finished our "honeymoon" by moving into the small quarters behind the main auditorium. That little parsonage was really a blessing in disguise! It was private and gave us a place to communicate where no one could hear our "discussions."

In many ways, Mineral was more like Nebraska than Seattle. It's a tiny town at the foot of Mount Rainier, almost an hour's drive from any big stores! The church was very small, maybe forty people, and poor. I'd play piano and Donald would preach. He always was an excellent preacher! I used to lead the adult Bible study. I didn't think anything of it at the time but imagine having an eighteen-year-old girl leading your Bible study! But the congregation was so kind and accepting of their new pastor and his very young wife. We loved the people and they loved us back.

Even in a tiny town like Mineral, God blessed our ministry. One Sunday, Donald was teaching about healing and how God still heals today, saying that we must believe and not doubt. In the middle of the sermon, a lady raised her hand and shouted, "My headache is gone!" Well, things like that will build a congregation's faith really quick! The church began to grow, and we saw the church double in size during our two years there. Our family grew, too, as we welcomed our firstborn son, Danny.

As I said before, the church couldn't afford to pay us much and we never had enough money; we frequently ran out of food. What would you do if you had a little baby in your arms and literally no food in your fridge? Would you start doubting God's call? Or His goodness? Would you be filled with fear? Call your parents and ask for money? For Donald and me, that was when we really learned to live by faith. We'd kneel and call out to God and even though our cupboard was still empty, we'd believe—in faith—that our prayers were answered. Do you know what would happen next? We'd hear a knock on the door and there would be a sack of groceries from someone in our congregation! We didn't know it then, but God was preparing us for an even bigger adventure of faith.

Faith PowerPoint: Thank God for the answer, before you actually see it.

So, do I regret pastoring such a small congregation? No! How could I regret learning those early lessons of faith and seeing God's provision right when we needed it?

CHAPTER 2

When Faith Becomes Active

⸺⸺⸺⸺⸺⸺ ୬୧ ⸺⸺⸺⸺⸺⸺

Two years after moving to Mineral, Donald and I attended that mission conference where he heard God's call to the Philippines. When we got back home, we looked up a map of the Philippines and felt God leading us to a city we'd never heard of before: Davao City, on the second largest island of Mindanao. We didn't know anyone there and weren't working with any mission agency, but we knew God was calling us.

After saying goodbye to our congregation, we spent the next year getting ready. We traveled around Washington and Oregon, trying to raise support. In the end, only one church agreed to support us: Broadway Tabernacle, where Donald had been an assistant pastor. They promised us $400 a month; that was all we had to live on and fund our ministry. We literally sold everything, including our car, to pay our way to the Philippines—we believed we'd spend the rest of our lives there, so no need to hang on to anything! We felt like Peter when he said:

> "Look, we have given up everything and followed You [becoming Your disciples and accepting You as Teacher and Lord]." Jesus said, "I assure you and most solemnly say to you, there is no one who has given up a house or brothers or sisters or mother or father or children or farms, for My sake and for the gospel's sake, who will not receive a hundred times as much now in the present age... (AMPC, Mark 10:28-30).

On a November morning, almost exactly one year after we said "yes" to God, Donald, two-year-old Danny, and I boarded a cargo ship docked at Pier 91 in downtown Seattle. It was just like in the movies—all our friends and family on the dock, waving goodbye.

Back in those days, commercial air travel wasn't very common, so freighters were the most economical way to cross the ocean. Cargo ships would typically have a few cabins set aside for passengers. They were a little nicer than the crew's quarters, but nothing like cruise ships today. There were about a dozen passengers on that trip. If I remember correctly, the rest of them were nuns. We ate our meals with the officers. It wasn't fancy, but I enjoyed it well enough and, of course, I made new friends!

Our cabin had a window overlooking the bow of the ship. As I said, it was November and we hit bad weather right away. This wasn't one of those huge 1,000-foot shipping containers like you would see today. It was only 300 feet long, so you can imagine what that was like! Donald and I would watch as we went over a huge wave, then the bow would tip down and we could only see water ahead. We'd head up the next wave and, for a moment, we just saw sky and then CRASH! we'd hit the water. I loved it—just another adventure! But my poor Donald got so seasick. Danny and I would go down to eat in the galley, and he'd stay in bed, absolutely miserable. He lost almost twenty pounds before we reached land!

When I tell people about our voyage, they're surprised that I wasn't afraid. We were headed to a strange land, without a sending agency or a detailed plan, where we didn't know anyone and didn't have any contacts (or so we thought). Second Corinthians 5:7 says, "We walk by faith and not by sight." And 4:18 says, "We consider and look not to the things that are seen but to things that are unseen!" That's easier said than done! Where did we find the faith to step out like that? God had spent the past three years teaching us to walk by faith. Every time we ran out of food at our first church and chose to pray instead of panic, we were learning to step out on faith. When we declared that we were going to the Philippines and Donald quit his job so we could prepare, we were activating our faith. When we walked onto that freighter, we were walking by faith.

On that voyage, we kept repeating Hebrews 11:8, "Abraham knew he was destined to receive an inheritance." He was our example, setting out to the Promised Land without knowing the way. Whenever we were afraid, we'd pray God's Word and repeat it out loud. As I said, you have to speak His Word out loud! The fear would rise up and we'd say, "We confidently say the Lord is my helper. I will not fear or be terrified!" (Hebrews 13:6). Faith isn't faith when you're walking by sight. Faith becomes great faith when you step out, when you trust God with all your heart and not lean on your own understanding (Proverbs 3:5-6).

Faith PowerPoint: Speaking God's Word activates faith!

Three weeks after leaving the cold and rainy Northwest, we arrived in the land of our calling. I'd done a lot of traveling, but I'd never experienced anything like Manila. It was forty degrees hotter than Seattle and more humid than an indoor pool. Filipino men ran along the wharf, shouting words I couldn't understand. As we walked down the gangway, there were almost too many new sights, sounds, and smells for me to take in. The dock was crowded with faces we'd never seen before, but we knew they were our future!

We stood there, unsure of what to do next. Doubts began to creep into Donald's spirit, and he felt the immensity of leading a young wife and child into this foreign land. But then a well-dressed Filippino woman approached us.

"Excuse me," she said in clear English. "Are there any Ostrom's on that ship?"

We were so shocked that it took a moment to respond.

"That's us!" Donald finally said.

The woman introduced herself as the governor's wife and welcomed us to the Philippines. She pinned a beautiful corsage on me then led the three of us to a black limousine. Her husband got out and greeted us, then said something to the customs officials and handed them some brightly colored pesos. The three of us got into the limo with the governor and his wife then we were driven to their mansion for a nice dinner. On the drive, he told us that his daughter was a student at the University of Washington. Donald and I remembered meeting her in Seattle but hadn't thought anything more of it. Well, she'd contacted her parents and asked them to meet us. God honored our faith and obedience!

CHAPTER 2

When Faith Becomes Active | 17

Faith PowerPoint: Faith always expects God to show up—always right on time!

After that, God provided again: We'd met another student in Washington whose father was a doctor in Tondo, Manila's largest neighborhood. We spent the next five weeks living with him, acclimating to the culture, taking care of visas, and waiting for our Jeep to clear customs. Tondo was largely a shantytown, well-known for crime, but I didn't care—just another adventure! It was probably a better place to prepare for our mission's work than the governor's mansion anyway.

We got on another freighter to Davao City, which was the third largest city in the Philippines. Once again, we got off the boat expecting not to know anyone. This time, we were greeted by a <u>Foursquare pastor who was a personal friend of Aimee Semple MacPherson (the founder of Foursquare)</u>. She helped us find our way around the city then we checked into the nicest hotel. This wasn't an extravagance. We'd been told that it was important to find a safe place where we could trust the food. Donald immediately began to look for our new home. A real estate agent showed him several places, but we said "no" to all of them. After two or three weeks at the hotel, watching our money dwindle, we asked God why He hadn't provided a place yet.

"I already have," He said. "But you refused it."

Immediately, we knew which one He meant. It was a nice place outside of town that we said was too expensive—$200 a month out of our monthly support of $400. God wanted to give us more than we dared hope for! We stepped out on faith and called the real estate agent. It was a wonderful home. Almost 2,500 square feet, maid's quarters over the garage, surrounded by a tall wall, and with a peaceful courtyard filled by guava, papaya, and palm trees. Danny and I had many fun-filled days playing in the courtyard!

God knew we needed that house as a place of refuge. As Americans, we were targets for theft. In fact, Donald lost a fair amount of money to a pickpocket in Manila! This house had black metal spikes lining the fence and we hired a "house boy" (as they were called) named Felix, a trustworthy young man in his mid-twenties who lived in the maid quarters. Everyone had either a maid or house boy because you could never leave your house unattended. Active faith knows that God is our refuge, but never confuses carelessness with faith!

Once we had a home, the next thing to find was a place for our church and God led us to the perfect place: a storefront right on Main Street in the business district. We called the church "Faith Tabernacle," in honor of our sending church, Broadway Tabernacle. We couldn't call it *Broadway* Tabernacle because the only Broadway they'd heard of in the Philippines was New York's

Broadway theaters. Besides, "Faith" seemed the perfect name to call our church, don't you think?

We bought pews and a piano, hung up a sign, and got everything set up. On Sunday mornings, we'd just throw the doors open. I'd start playing the piano and Donald would sing. This wasn't like America where everyone pretends they aren't interested and kind of hangs around outside the door. No, the Filipinos would just walk in to see what those Americans were doing! Then Donald would start preaching the Gospel through an interpreter (though most of them understood English well enough). It was such a wonderful atmosphere and people loved being there. We started with two people and over the next three years, grew to a church of 300!

Leaders have a way of rising up, so we'd watch for leaders that we could train and release into ministry. Donald would bring these young men into our house to disciple them and teach them the Word. I have many wonderful memories of these young men sitting in our house, learning to read the Bible and praying in faith.

Just like when we were back at our first church, we frequently found ourselves on our knees asking God to provide for us, then thanking Him—by faith—for the answer we knew would come. Sometimes we'd received an unexpected gift by wire. Or the money would arrive, just in time, with a letter from home. Back in those days, it took two weeks to get letters, so that meant that God had literally provided the money before we asked. We just had to wait for His answer!

Our three years in the Philippines were very happy and I was content to live the rest of my life serving God in the land of our calling. But that's not to say it was always easy. We had to learn to choose joy over fear, even in the face of death threats.

So, do I regret the storms (sometimes literal!) of being missionaries in the Philippines? No, because sometimes we must go through storms to make it to the other side of victory!

CHAPTER 3

Choosing Joy over Fear

⁓꙳⁓

Joy is my middle name, given to me by my grateful parents. After Norma Jean was born, my parents were told they wouldn't be able to have any more children. So when I came along, they were so happy that they put "Joy" in my name. But just because joy is part of my name, it doesn't mean that it comes naturally!

One Sunday, a young man named Pat came into our church and listened to the message. God touched his heart and Donald led him to salvation. That was always so exciting for us. It was for that very purpose that we'd given our lives to the Philippines! A couple days later, we were resting at home when the phone rang. Donald leapt up to answer. We were always happy to get a phone call, whether from back home or from one of our friends in the Philippines. I vividly remember watching his expression turn from joy to concern as he listened to the voice on the other end.

"You messed up our friend, Pat," the voice said. "He belongs to the Communist Party and we won't allow you to take him. We know where you live and we're going to kill you!"

As soon as Donald hung up, we knelt down and began to pray. We were facing a great test of faith. Do we live in fear for our lives or choose to be joyful because Pat had been born again? We chose joy! Fear does not produce joy, so we kept repeating God's Word—just as we had on the freighter, "Fear not! I will never leave you – never forsake you! No never." We knew that God had called us to the Philippines and He would take care of us! We prayed from John 10:10, "The devil comes to steal, kill and destroy our joy, our peace, our safety, but Jesus came to give us abundant life."

How could we choose joy in the face of death threats? Because choosing joy is an act of *faith* and God had already been building our faith in so many ways. Faith is faith in every area of our lives. The same God who provided groceries in Mineral, Washington promised to protect us in Davao City, Philippines.

Faith PowerPoint: Joy is an attitude of faith in God and His Word.

That is not to say we ignored the threat. As God's Word says, "We are not stupid or ignorant of Satan's devices" (2 Corinthians 2:11). We were cautious and immediately put Felix (our house boy) on alert, telling him to carefully guard our gate and watch for any strange visitors. But we held on to God's promises and spoke them out loud. I want to say that again: it's very important to say the Word, not just think it. We will have what we say! As Mark 11:23 says,

> Truly I tell you, whoever _says_ to this mountain, Be lifted up and thrown into the sea! and does not doubt at all in his heart but believes that what he _says_ will take place, it will be done for him (AMPC, emphasis added).

Another time that I was tempted to choose fear over joy was when I realized that I'd be giving birth to our second child in the Philippines. The birth of a child should be a joy-filled event, but being so far from home—where the medical care was below what we had in the States—gave me many reasons to be worried. It was even harder because my mother had passed away about six months after we'd moved to the Philippines. In spite of everything, I chose joy, knowing God would be with me.

Here is a funny—and embarrassing—little story: The Filipino women would ask our son Danny if he wanted a brother or sister (back then, you had to wait for the birth to find out). He'd respond, "I don't care, so long as it's white." That was so embarrassing! But you have to remember, he'd been playing with the Filipino children for a couple of years and just wanted someone who looked like him. Incidentally, Doug was the whitest of all four of my babies!

Choosing joy over fear is a never-ending battle. Even as I write, I'm hearing rioting and looting very close to my home. Once again, I'm challenged to "fear not" and repeat God's Word:

> I will say of the Lord, He is my Refuge and my Fortress, my God; on Him I lean and rely, and in Him I [confidently] trust!
> Because you have made the Lord your refuge, and the Most High your dwelling place, there shall no evil befall you, nor any plague or calamity come near your tent (AMPC, Psalm 91:2, 9-10).

Fear destroys joy. Also as I write this, a worldwide virus has become a terror for millions. People are wearing masks and staying in their home out of fear. When I first heard about this, Psalm 91:5-7 rose out of my spirit:

> You shall not be afraid of the terror of the night, nor of the arrow (the evil plots and slanders of the wicked) that flies by day, nor of the pestilence that stalks in darkness, nor of the destruction and sudden death that surprise and lay waste at noonday.

> A thousand may fall at your side, and ten thousand at your right hand, but it shall not come near you (AMPC).

That's a command: "You shall not be afraid"! Every morning, I began to repeat this out loud, saying, "No virus will come near my dwelling!" I know it sounds like bragging, but I'm only repeating God's Word!

Faith PowerPoint: To hold onto our joy, we must repeat God's Word concerning our circumstances.

I loved our three years in the Philippines. Planting churches, teaching pastors, and seeing Filipinos saved every Sunday! I never wanted this season to end and couldn't imagine that God was about to do "superabundantly, far over and above all that we dare ask or imagine" (Ephesians 3:20), especially because it began with one of the most painful seasons of my life.

So, do I regret refusing to give into fear from a death threat? The devil will try any obstacle to discourage obedience. Thank God he was defeated when Jesus died on the cross!

CHAPTER 4

Entering A New Season

 ᘐ ᕲ ᕲ ᖱ

Life consists of always changing seasons. Some new seasons are obvious and some are subtle, but they always begin with something changing: your circumstances, a new challenge in business, making new friends, leaving old ones, or moving to a new location or church. Sometimes a new season begins with a big new step in our walk with God.

New seasons always provide us with an opportunity to grow in faith. Why? Because our natural response to change (even good change!) is fear. If we give into fear, we will never grow and always be stuck. To put it bluntly, it's the losers in life that refuse to leave the old season and enter the new one.

So, how do we find the faith to embrace new seasons? Knowing and quoting God's Word! In the first chapter,

I told you about when Jesus, in Mark 4:35, declared the disciples' future: "Let us go to the other side!" They didn't know their journey would take them through a storm, but He did. Jesus promised to get them to the other side, and He promises us the same, for "Jesus Christ is the same yesterday, today, and forever" (Hebrews 13:8). So, we can boldly say:

> The Lord is my Helper [in time of need], I will not be afraid. "What will man do to me?" (AMPC, Hebrews 13:6).

Faith PowerPoint: Embrace new seasons with faith, not fear!

On August 24, 1961, Donald and I began our longest and most intense season. I was six months pregnant with our third son, Larry. Donald's 31st birthday was coming up, so we decided we deserved a special treat! We left Danny and Doug (now six and two) with a trusted friend and went out for dinner at a nice hotel. As we were eating, the manager came to our table and said, "Excuse me, Mrs. Ostrom. You have a phone call at the front desk."

Donald and I followed him, and I took the phone from the manager. Back in those days, international phone calls were very low quality (this was long before fiber optics); I had to press my ear into the phone to hear over the hissing. That is how I heard the news. My beloved father had been flying home from one of his nursing homes in Iowa. My dear sister had been with him—all she had ever wanted to do was serve God and help our dad. The plane had gone down in a remote area outside of Seattle, killing everyone on board the four-seater Cessna.

At first, the news wouldn't set in. It seemed impossible that they wouldn't ever come visit Donald and I and see all the work we'd done in the Philippines, that they would never meet Doug. That there wouldn't be any more letters from them. Never again would I see my father or hear my sister play the piano. Not until heaven, would the Horton family be reunited.

Air travel was becoming more common, so I was able to get a flight for Doug and me on a cargo plane out of Davao City to attend the funeral. Imagine that! Twenty-four years old, six months pregnant and holding a two-year-old's hand as we made our way through a total of four airports, then trying to get comfortable on an old-fashioned turboprop. Transpacific flights took longer back then—twenty-six hours—so I had lots of time to think.

I was just numb. It happens so fast, when you get bad news like that. It's hard to even comprehend what was happening, let alone think about the future. I struggled to believe there could ever possibly be a good future. In times like that, God's Word becomes your bottom line. I chose to filter everything through my "faith thinking."

Right there on that plane, I spoke Jeremiah 29:11 out loud:

> For I know the thoughts and plans that I have for you, says the Lord, thoughts and plans for welfare and peace and not for evil, to give you hope in your final outcome (AMPC).

And then Proverbs 3:5-6:

> Lean on, trust in, and be confident in the Lord with all your heart and mind and do not rely on your own insight or understanding. In all your ways know, recognize, and acknowledge Him, and He will direct and make straight and plain your paths (AMPC).

We didn't know how long I'd be gone. I was the only surviving family member, so suddenly my family's entire estate—including his thriving nursing home business spanning four states—was now my responsibility. Our plan was that Donald and Danny would remain behind to continue our ministry in the Philippines. I'd sell the business and return to the Philippines as soon as possible. We just wanted everything to go back to "normal." So when I got on that plane, I couldn't have imagined how much our lives and ministry were going to change.

There are many who would say that the plane crash was an attack of the enemy. I don't believe it for a moment. So long as we're living in God's will (and I know my father was a great man of faith), the enemy can't touch us. I didn't understand why it happened, but I knew God would use it, so I had to ask Him for wisdom.

In the days that followed, I really came to comprehend Isaiah 46:10, "I declare the end and result from the beginning... My counsel shall stand and I will do all my pleasure and purpose!" Even in the midst of sorrow, I found great comfort remembering that God is never taken by surprise. He knows every season we'll go through before we're even born!

> Your eyes have seen my unformed substance; and in Your book were all written the days that were appointed for me, when as yet there was not one of them [even taking shape] (AMP, Psalm 139:16).

Dad had attended Philadelphia Church, a wonderful charismatic church in Seattle. Their pastor, Roy Johnson, presided over the funeral, which was held graveside at the cemetery in northern Seattle. My father was a well-respected man, not just by Christians but also by secular business leaders. He had an all-too-rare combination of integrity, devotion to Jesus, a kind and gentle manner, and great business sense.

Everything in my life changed after his death. I went from renting a place in the Philippines to owning a very nice house in Magnolia, one of Seattle's best neighborhoods. I went from dirt roads, palm trees, and jeepneys (brightly painted minibuses that had been converted from surplus WWII jeeps), to boulevards, pine trees, and owning my father's two cars. By today's standards, I'd gone from being a poor missionary to being a millionaire. More importantly, I was now in charge of the family business. I'd grown up working with my father, so I wasn't completely lost. But it was still a huge challenge. In addition to constantly praying for Donald and Danny and our mission work, I was now asking God for the wisdom to run a business that stretched from the Northwest to the Midwest.

The first thing I did was meet with all the facility administrators, even having to fly the same route where my father and sister had died. <u>Fortunately, he was always careful to hire very capable leaders;</u> without them, there was no way I could've accomplished it all. Even still, I was stretched very thin. After <u>six weeks</u>, Donald told me he just couldn't handle being apart anymore. He decided to leave a trusted Filipino in charge of the ministry and came back home until we could sell the business and return to our "real" calling. (See how hard it can be to enter a new season?)

I picked Donald and Danny up from the newly renovated SeaTac airport (it had been expanded in response to the booming air travel industry). I was happy to see them, of course, but I was also ready for some help! I was almost eight months pregnant, raising Doug, and running the family business. Even though I considered myself to be a very capable woman, it would be wonderful to lean on my "helpmate" as we prepared the business for sale. For as long as I'd known Donald, he'd had smart business sense (my father wasn't just being nice when he offered him a job).

You might think that moving back to America would be hard for Danny, after living half his life in the Philippines, but kids don't have much of a problem adjusting. Donald was the one that struggled. I could tell more than half his heart was still back in Davao City. As desperately as I needed his help, I knew he needed time to adjust. Larry was born six weeks later, which of course was a blessing, but only added to my exhaustion. But rather than accepting this new season, Donald did everything he could to act like he was still a missionary. Instead of helping me with the business, he spent so many nights holding meetings at our church. He seemed lost without his ministry and part of me felt bad for him, but a much bigger part was getting very angry. I was supposed to be a stay-at-home mom, with two active boys and a newborn, but Donald still expected me to deal with the family business and was getting frustrated that it was taking so long to sell!

I felt abandoned by my husband and would sometimes lash out at him. Our home was filled with strife. All I could do was pray that Donald would have a change of heart. What I didn't know was that it was a spiritual battle—Satan's lies about money and business were preventing us from entering a prosperous new season. Believe it or not, it took a man of God yelling at my husband to break us free from those lies!

So, do I regret being far away when my family was killed in a plane crash? No! if I hadn't obeyed His call to go to the Philippines, I could've been on the plane with them.

CHAPTER 5

A Life-Changing Conversation

—————⟶ ๑ ๑ ๑ ⟵—————

Satan loves to twist God's Word and turn it into lies. He even tried to do that with Jesus! (Matthew 4:5-7). And what did Jesus do? He quoted Scripture right back at him! We have to study the full counsel of God in order to withstand the devices of the Enemy. That's what was happening to Donald; Satan kept whispering into his ear, "Money is the root of all evil!" Then he'd say, "It's harder for a camel to go through the eye of a needle than a rich man to be saved." Satan deliberately ignored everything the Bible said about God's blessings and how to use them to bless others.

Donald had grown up in poverty and had never studied what the Bible said about God's earthly blessings, so he was easily deceived. Not only did he believe wealth was ungodly, he'd also been taught that you had to choose between a "secular job" or ministry, and that ministry was the godly choice. That was so different from my childhood, watching my father use his business to build churches! Donald knew he was called to build the Kingdom of God and was genuinely afraid of "selling out" like other pastors had. His attitude was, "I'm not letting this business or money destroy me!"

Because I was going through so much and felt so abandoned, I didn't see the battle Donald was going through. I was used to working with my husband and I hated how it felt like we were working against each other. I just prayed that the business would quickly sell. But settling an estate and selling a large business is very complicated. It took almost a year for God to answer my prayers, but He did it differently than I expected and used an unlikely source—a world famous evangelist.

T. L. Osborn may not be a well-known name in America, but around the world he was almost as well-known as Billy Graham. He would preach to crowds as large as 300,000 and held crusades throughout Europe, Asia, and Africa. Just like in the early church, God would confirm his message through signs and wonders. Thousands of people were healed through his ministry.

Donald and I had known T. L. Osborn through our work in the Philippines. We'd been handing out his evangelistic tracts and needed to get more. Almost everything was done by mail in those days, and when Donald wrote to place the order, he asked T. L. Osborn if he'd be interested in holding a crusade in Davao City. Long story short, T. L. Osborn said, "Yes," and we rented a spot by the post office that held 3,000 people. We became instant friends with T. L. Osborn and his wife, Daisy. They came over to our house for dinner, something they never did. I remember buying ground beef and making spaghetti because I thought that was a good American meal! We had a great time of fellowship and became very close.

Anyway, T. L. Osborn came to Seattle for an event, so of course we offered to pick him up from the airport. I will never forget that drive! T. L. Osborn asked Donald how we were doing and Donald was practically apologetic about us not being on the mission field. Then he said something that really irritated me,"I'm still a minister, not a businessman. That's why Marlene is in charge of the business."

Donald thought that would impress T. L. Osborn, but he was completely wrong! T. L. Osborn looked at Donald in shock then shouted, "Don Ostrom, get off your butt and take over that business!"

I stifled a laugh as T. L. Osborn explained a "totally new" idea to Donald: He could be a godly businessman and a wealthy Christian and use his money to build far more churches in the Philippines than we could on $400 a month!

God used T. L. Osborn's rebuke to totally change Donald's perspective. It didn't happen overnight. He still didn't like to think of himself as a businessman, not until he heard God say to him, "Son, it makes no difference to me if people call you a preacher or businessman. Just do My will, and you bring the highest glory to My name." By telling him that, God removed the false belief that business and ministry must be separate. After that, Donald finally put his whole heart into this new season.

Faith PowerPoint: God doesn't care if you're in ministry or business—He just wants you to do His will right where you are!

Looking back, it's amazing how God used that one little conversation to change everything. It gave us a brand-new revelation of God's reason for prospering us—so we could give more away! As God said to Abraham,

> "...indeed, I will greatly bless you, and I will greatly multiply your descendants like the stars of the heavens and like the sand on the seashore; and your seed shall possess the gate of their enemies [as conquerors]. Through your seed all the nations of the earth shall be blessed, because you have heard and obeyed My voice" (AMPC, Genesis 22:17-18).

Prosperity comes from God. Third John 1:2 says, "Beloved, I pray that you may prosper in every way and [that your body] may keep well, even as [I know] your soul keeps well and prospers" (AMPC) and Psalms 35:27

A blessing

says that God takes pleasure in the prosperity of His servant. All of that is God's Word! But God blesses us in order to be a blessing to others. This is a fundamental principle—He doesn't prosper us so we can live easy and buy a nicer car or a bigger house. No! He blesses us so that His blessings can pour freely, through us, to the poor and the lost.

This was a whole new way of thinking for us. We'd "forgotten" that Jesus's command to go into all the world requires lots of money! Then Acts 20:35 says, "It is more blessed to give than to receive." Accepting God's blessings didn't lessen our need to live by faith (just the opposite—Donald liked to say that our acts of faith now required more zeros behind it!) nor change our commitment to missions. But now we sought to be as prosperous as possible in order to bless others and help fulfill the Great Commission.

Donald met with each of our facility administrators (all of whom were Christians) and basically said, "Our goal is to make money in order to support the Kingdom of God." And that's what we did. Donald ran the business well (I'll tell you more about that in the next chapter) and we were able to fly back to the Philippines two or three times a year. Instead of one church in Davao City, we literally founded a thousand throughout the Philippines. And many of these churches went on to establish churches of their own, making it impossible for us to count the real number!

One of the most important things we did in the Philippines was start a Bible school. Donald taught new pastors how to preach, lead a church, and (most importantly) he taught them the Word—new churches absolutely must be founded on God's Word. We taught these pastors to begin preaching on tithing as soon as they started a church. They had to become self-supporting right away. We were happy to help them financially at the beginning, but we refused to keep giving.

When you raise your children, you're happy to support them. But when they grow up, it's healthier for them to take care of themselves. That's what we'd tell the pastors, "Your church is 'old enough' now. Teach your people to give because it's time to support yourself." This is crucial for many reasons: It's healthier for the church and it keeps them from becoming dependent on us. It allowed their congregation to experience the blessings that come from tithing and giving. And it allowed us to use that money to start another church. This principle allowed us to start a thousand healthy, independent churches instead of a handful of needy ones!

Not long after that life-changing conversation with T. L. Osborne, Donald heard about a group called "Full Gospel Businessmen's Fellowship International"

(FGBMI). They hosted breakfast meetings for Christian businessmen committed to sharing the gospel. For the first time in his life, Donald was surrounded by Spirit-filled men who excelled at business and ministry. It was at these meetings that he got to know Fred Doerflein, owner of Northwest Piano and Organ.

Fred invited us to attend the international conference in Seattle. Donald and I were so <u>inspired by listening to wealthy businessmen testify about prospering and helping the poor.</u> Such a different perspective than "money is the root of all evil!" The conference ended with a banquet held at the Space Needle and we sat with John and Dodie Osteen, founders of Lakewood Church in Houston. When John passed away in 1999, their youngest son Joel took over as pastor and has gone on to have a well-known ministry.

We became very close friends with John and Dodie. On one occasion, Donald invited John to see our work in the Philippines and that trip really impacted him. Lakewood church went on to have a huge emphasis on missions, sending out many long-term and short-term missionaries. John and Dodie later invited us to visit them in Houston and had us stand up in front of the congregation and said, "This is the man that introduced me to world missions."

FGBMI became a very important part of our lives for many years. We'd host large banquets, invite Christian businessmen, then challenge them to prosper and use their money for God. We had hundreds of men (sometimes even a thousand!) at these banquets. Donald also pioneered the Seattle chapter (which was the largest in the world) and served as FGBMI's international vice-president for many years.

Of course, there is far more to pleasing God than using the profits for missions. It didn't matter how much money we raised if we didn't operate the business in a godly manner. In the next chapter, I want to tell you more about running a business by faith.

So, do I regret growing health care facilities to provide extraordinary care for seniors instead of being a missionary? In addition to providing for God's work, we fulfilled my father's desire to care for people in the last years of their life. Truly a great calling!

CHAPTER 6

God's Business

———— ༠༦༠ ————

One time, Donald and I were visiting our Port Orchard facility and he told the staff about all the charitable work being done with the business's profits. A couple of days later, one of the nurses was talking to the administrator.

"It's nice to give all that money to God," she said. "But how about giving some of it to the employees?"

The administrator passed that on to Donald and it hit him really hard. Then he was reading in James,

> [But] look! [Here are] the wages that you have withheld by fraud from the laborers who have reaped your fields, crying out [for vengeance]; and the cries of the harvesters have come to the ears of the Lord of hosts (AMPC, James 5:4).

Donald was great at taking the Word and applying it to his life. He knew that he wasn't withholding wages by fraud, but he believed God was telling us to increase

45

all 500 employees' salaries by 50%! He told the administrators about his plan and they gasped. "You can't do that, Don! You've seen our reports, you know we can't afford it," they said.

<u>Obedient faith doesn't always look good on paper, but Donald knew what God told him to do and responded with active faith.</u> "The Bible says that he who helps the poor lends to the Lord [Proverbs 19:17]. God will repay us," he said. "Anyway, I'm the boss and we're doing it!"

When we told the employees about the raise, they applauded us. We knew those raises would make a huge difference in their lives. God did repay us; our profits didn't drop one bit! And because of our generosity, our employees were extremely loyal. Some of our employees were with us for over thirty years. Everyone wanted to come work for us and we had a far lower turnover rate than other nursing homes.

Many Christian business leaders are so worried about the bottom line that they ignore God's promises. They don't carry their faith into their offices. They might sing loudly and raise their hands high on Sunday morning, but the rest of the week they cut sharp deals, skirt the law, and greedily hang on to every penny.

Even though Donald had grown up studying God's Word and had spent years teaching it to others, he always continued to read the Word. We'd attend conferences and read books that built up our faith (we were friends with faith teacher and preacher Kenneth E. Hagin and Donald served on his board for twenty-five years). We'd read books and listen to sermon tapes to help us grow. But Donald wasn't just a hearer of the Word, he was a doer. As I said, he was very good at reading the Word and applying it to every area of his life and business.

Because of his commitment to applying the Word, Donald and I developed many core values for success, including:

- Keep your priorities right; don't allow the business to rob you of time with your spouse and children.
- Speak faith and success over your business and employees. Be assured that God wants you to prosper and succeed. (One time, a facility administrator said, "We just can't get good employees." Donald responded, "Don't ever say that again! We will always have good employees." <u>He wouldn't let our administrator speak out of fear and doubt.</u>)
- Pray for God's protection and resist fear through knowledge of God's Word.
- Seek godly counsel and advice.

- Expect excellence, honesty, and diligence from yourself first and then your employees.
- Maintain inner purity. Run from immorality—lust and adultery will rob you of everything!
- Honor employees with fairness and respect. No favoritism. No threats.
- Be willing to change, or you will lose momentum and eventually your business will fail.
- Maintain an attitude of humility.

But there were four guiding principles that were especially important to us. The first one was *generosity*. As God's Word says,

> There is the one who [generously] scatters [abroad], and yet increases all the more; And there is the one who withholds what is justly due, but it results only in want and poverty (AMP, Proverbs 11:24).

Donald once had a CPA tell him he could easily make more money. We had too many nurses, he said. We should fire a bunch of them. He also wanted us to let go of our long-term staff and replace them with lower paid people, like other facilities did. But our bottom line wasn't profits. It was running a business that honored God, both by giving to His work and by taking excellent care of our guests. By being generous in this way, we had a very good reputation and gained many residents who were transferred out of facilities that put money first.

Our second guiding principle was *trust*. This first of all meant trusting God. Because we operated our business to honor Him, we knew we could look to God to prosper and protect it. Every day, we thanked Him and spoke His Word over our business. And we didn't do anything without praying and asking God for wisdom.

One of the most important things we trusted Him for was good employees. This was something I learned from my father—be very, very careful who you hire, especially your administrators. He hired a lot of ex-pastors. They made the best administrators because they loved people. That's what we wanted in our administrators—people that would love the residents, put them first, and pray over them.

"Trust" also meant trusting our administrators. A lot of people asked how we could fly to the Philippines and go on so many missions trips. It was because we trusted our administrators and put real responsibility on their shoulders. That's really important. A lot of business owners try to control everything and their employees are left to wonder if they're trusted or not. Our administrators had the authority to make decisions. Sure, they made some mistakes, but so did we! And because they were given a share of the profits, they treated it as their own business. We also rewarded them well for their work, including letting them lease a new Cadillac every two years.

Our third guiding principle was *faithfulness*. To me, faithfulness is a characteristic of a successful person. This means being faithful in every area of your life. Faithful with your business obligations. Absolutely faithful to your spouse and your family. But what about being faithful to your church? In Psalm 92:13, God's Word promises that those who are planted in the house of the Lord will flourish.

This is not a popular thing to say, but how can Christian businessmen and women "neglect the assembly of the saints" (Hebrews 10:25) and still expect God to prosper them? We raised our four boys in church, every Sunday morning, Wednesday night, and Friday night. This was before nurseries were a thing, so they'd just play underneath the pews. More than once, I'd find them chewing gum that they hadn't brought with them! But they all grew up healthy. More than that, all four of them are still committed to a local church.

Our pastor always knew that he could count on Donald and Marlene being in church, supporting and encouraging him. Whenever there was some crisis or controversy, the congregation would see us there, supporting the pastor. This isn't popular either but being faithful in church also means submitting to your pastor. God's Word says,

Obey your spiritual leaders and submit to them [continually recognizing their authority over you], for they are constantly keeping watch over your souls and guarding your spiritual welfare, as men who will have to render an account [of their trust] (AMPC, Hebrews 13:17).

Pastors are God's gift to us. Even when they are younger and less experienced than we are, they are still God's gift. We listened to our pastors. We followed their suggestions and met with them often. Donald and I may have been in ministry longer, preached more sermons, traveled more, and had more money, but we always had a spirit of submission. Be sure to choose your pastor very carefully and seek the Spirit for guidance but once you find a pastor, you need to submit. As the Bible says, God opposes the proud but shows favor to the humble (James 4:6). How can you expect God to bless you if you're too proud to submit to your pastor?

Faith PowerPoint: Successful people have a spirit of submission.

Another important part of being faithful is honoring the Sabbath. Donald would never work on Sunday. God gave it to us as a day of rest. It was for our own benefit, for our health, enjoyment, and prosperity. Sometimes you don't have a choice about working on Sunday, especially if you work for someone else. But you still need to take off a full day each week in order to rest, get into the Word, and seek God. It's the fourth commandment—six days you shall work and on the seventh you rest. This is a gift for happiness and health. By the way, this applies to pastors just as much as business people.

It's easy to believe that you're too busy and can't afford to take a day off. With running a large business across several states, Donald could have used that excuse almost every Sunday. But he didn't. We believed God's promise to provide above and beyond what we would have made had he worked on Sunday. Honoring the Sabbath is an act of faith.

Faith PowerPoint: You can do more in six days with God's blessing than seven days without it!

Being faithful also means tithing. In fact, this is the first step to prospering and living a generous and obedient life. That's one of the reasons we told our Filipino pastors to start preaching on it right away. As God's Word says,

> You are cursed with the curse, for you are robbing Me, even this whole nation. Bring all the tithes (the whole tenth of your income) into the storehouse, that there may be food in My house, and prove Me now by it, says the Lord of hosts, if I will not open the windows of heaven for you and pour you out a blessing, that there shall not be room enough to receive it. And I

will rebuke the devourer…for your sakes and he shall not destroy the fruits of your ground, neither shall your vine drop its fruit before the time in the field, says the Lord of hosts. And all nations shall call you happy and blessed, for you shall be a land of delight, says the Lord of hosts (AMPC, Malachi 3:9-12).

When Donald and I were preparing to move to the Philippines, God led us into an evangelism ministry that had us traveling around in a little camping trailer. Finances were very tight and we needed every cent for food and gas, so Donald decided we couldn't afford to tithe. That was a bad decision!

A couple weeks later, we were invited to lead a crusade at a church on the Oregon coast. We hit some heavy traffic in Portland and Donald took a corner too sharply. The trailer caught the front of another car and had a three-foot hole torn in it. That evening, he complained to God. "Here I am serving you. Why did you let this happen to me?"

God reminded him that he'd withheld the tithe—that's what had opened the door for "the devourer." Donald immediately repented and promised never to do that again. When the church took an offering for us, he immediately repaid God for the missing tithe. We were glad to be obedient again, but there was still a hole in the trailer. After the meetings, we returned to his parents' house in southern Washington. While we were there, a friend fixed our trailer, as good as new, for free! Donald and I praised God for His grace and faithfulness to us, even when we had disobeyed.

Ever since then, Donald and I have tithed faithfully—a whole 10%—on all of our income in any form, including gifts, donations, and offerings taken for us. We set up a special bank account and had our administrators deposit 10% of their facilities profits directly into it.

Everything we have comes from God. It is all His. Tithing is just returning some of His money back by giving it into the storehouses, i.e. the place you are spiritually fed. When you fail to tithe, you are holding on to God's possessions and robbing Him. And God's Word is very clear—if you rob Him, you are under a curse. If you are faithful, you will be blessed.

One day, the Lord gave me the revelation that we are only stewards of God's prosperity. Everything I own belongs to Him. He is the Creator, and I am the caretaker. First Corinthians 10:26 says, "For the whole earth is the Lord's and everything in it." But we are only commanded to give Him 10% of our possessions; generosity is what we do above and beyond that!

Faith PowerPoint: Tithing doesn't count as generosity!

Our fourth guiding principle was _good record keeping._ The book of Proverbs is filled with godly wisdom both for a victorious life and a successful business, including this command to pay close attention to your assets:

> Be diligent to know the state of your flocks, and look well to your herds; for riches are not forever; does a crown endure to all generations? (AMPC Proverbs 27:27).

There's that saying about being "so heavenly minded that you're of no earthly good." Some Christians are so focused on things above that they don't pay attention to the things of this life. They separate business from ministry. But our lives are not our own. Everything we have comes from Him and everything we own belongs to Him. Since our lives are not our own, then neither is our business.

Because our business belonged to God, we felt a great responsibility to prosper. Not for our own benefit but for God's work. Remember, being in business wasn't something we'd asked for; we just wanted to be missionaries. We never forgot our calling. What I'm saying is that running a business isn't separate from our walk with God. In fact, Jesus said that how we handle our business and wealth will prove our trustworthiness with more important things:

> So if you have not been trustworthy in handling worldly wealth, who will trust you with true riches? (NIV Luke 16:1).

That's why it was so important to be responsible with our business. Every month, we received detailed reports about our "flocks." They broke down wages, occupancy levels, food and laundry costs, maintenance, etc. Donald would carefully study these reports and discuss any questions with the facility administrators. Trusting our managers didn't mean lack of oversight; paying attention to the reports allowed us both to trust them and to know what issues needed our full attention.

Ignoring the facts isn't a sign of faith. Paying close attention to the facts shows us where to apply our faith. Instead of just praying general prayers for God's blessing, reading the reports allowed us to pray specifically—with faith!—for specific needs. For instance, in the nursing home business, every empty bed meant money being lost. Whenever the reports showed too many empty beds, Donald and I would join hands and pray for that facility and declare those beds filled.

Faith PowerPoint: Ignoring facts is not faith.

I want to end this chapter with an encouraging word: I've talked about Mark 4:35, where Jesus said, "Let us go to the other side." Even though the disciples had to go through a huge storm to get there, they should've been confident because Jesus was in the boat with them. Storms happen in our professional lives just as much as our personal lives. But if your business is truly God's business, then you can also be confident that Jesus is with you in the boat. He's declared your future and will get you to the other side!

Our son, Doug, now runs our business and it still faces storms. The COVID-19 virus is obviously a huge danger for nursing homes. And we recently had a leak that caused $50,000 worth of damage that wasn't covered by insurance. These are the storms we have to face, but we know—by faith—that we'll come through them victoriously. We will not give into the devil's lies. We will not give into discouragement. We will not give into any kind of fear. Yes, that's easier said than done. But that is why I continue to read God's Word and speak His promises out loud.

Some of my greatest storms, and greatest joys, came from raising four boys. In fact, the longest storm of my life came from our own prodigal son. But it's in the storms that we really learn to pray. In the next couple of chapters, I want to share some of the lessons I've learned about prayer and taking authority over the devil.

So, do I regret running my business God's way, choosing generosity and faith over profits? I have no regrets! For "the blessing of the Lord brings true riches and He adds no sorrow to it" (Proverbs 10:22).

CHAPTER 7

Raising Our Boys

⸱୬୨୭⸱

As you'll remember, my son Larry was born shortly after we returned from the Philippines. Two years later, Paul was born. Four sons in eight years! We were done after that. Shortly before Paul was born, Donald and I bought a house in Fall City, about half an hour east of Seattle. The town was named after Snoqualmie Falls, a 268 foot waterfall just upriver from our house. We had fifty-two acres on the Snoqualmie River and a large rambler with a big living room, playroom, and a barn that held our goats.

It was the perfect place to raise four active boys. People sometimes ask if I wished for at least one daughter. I say, "No, girls are too picky!" and laugh. I think God gives us what we can handle, and boys were perfect for me (and I now have four wonderful daughters-in-law who have been such an encouragement). We had so many great adventures in that house. It was such a rewarding season for Donald and me. The boys loved growing up in the woods—hours and hours spent outdoors, running with their dogs, building forts, wrestling, floating down the river, riding motorbikes, or swimming in our pool.

As I said before, we established the habit of being in church. Sometimes four times a week! It was never a question of "if" we would go. It was always, "We will go!" The reward is that, to this very day, all four of our sons faithfully attend a local church. As Proverbs 22:6 says, "Train up a child in the way that he should go, and when he is old he will not depart from it." Of course, this doesn't always go as smoothly as we'd wish. I'll tell you more about that shortly.

Parenting was filled with joy, but also with the challenges of training, disciplining, and refereeing the four boys. But we always, always expressed our love for them. Like my father, Donald wasn't one of those harsh or distant fathers; even when he had to spank them, he'd always end by saying how much he loved them. When children know they are loved, they want to please us. We expressed our love with words, actions, attitudes, and lots of smiles. One rule we never broke was, "We will eat one meal together as a family every day!" And eating around the TV didn't count. I wish every family did this. Don't underestimate the importance of eating together! Some of our best conversations happened around the table.

Disciplining is very important, but there are more ways to handle a problem than just spanking. TVs stations were still a big deal back then and taking away the TV was very effective. One night, after the boys had lost their TV privileges, the Lord woke me up around midnight. I checked their beds and one of them was empty. I found one of the boys down the hall, watching a movie. He was surprised I'd caught him, but I said, "God woke me up; you can't get away with things like this." That made a real impression on him!

There were always plenty of opportunities for me to get mad or discouraged. I discovered that the best reaction was to keep my sense of humor and learn to see the funny side as often as possible. Like the time the boys talked me into riding their motorbike. It took off, straight for the trees, with me barely hanging on. I was dumped in the bushes and faced with a choice—get mad and tell them to stop laughing at me or else laugh with them! I chose joy and my boys still chuckle at the memory. Not overreacting saved me from much unnecessary and unhelpful conflict. As Proverbs 15:1 says, "A soft answer turns away wrath, but grievous words stir up anger" (AMPC).

So many people worry about every little danger their children could possibly face. We were never careless, but prayed God's protection over them, trusting Him to keep them safe and healthy. One time, when Larry was seven or eight, he snuck some matches and was playing with them in the woods behind the house. The next morning, we woke up to smoke coming out from the trees. He'd started a little bonfire and left it burning all night long! We rushed out and smothered it just in time—God was really protecting us that day.

As I was raising our boys, there were many times the devil whispered in my spirit, "These boys aren't going to serve God when they grow up. Just look at their generation—rebellious, mean, selfish, and lustful sinners." That's just like him, to attack us where we are already filled with doubts. The devil tells us lies that hit at our deepest fears:

- "You can't do anything. You won't amount to anything."
- "You aren't worthy of God's love or blessings."
- "No one likes you. You'll always be lonely."
- "God won't listen to your prayers—look how you've been acting lately."

If we listen to his lies and have a "victim" mentality, it's very hard to rise up against the enemy. That's why he keeps telling us those lies. But what does God's Word say? Jesus defeated the devil on the cross and he has no power over us! We need to arm ourselves with the revelation that God has disarmed him:

> [God] disarmed the principalities and powers that were ranged against us and made a bold

display and public example of them, in triumphing over them in Him and in it [the cross] (AMPC Colossians 2:15).

Not only that, but His Word says that He "set a table before me in the presence of my enemy" (Psalm 23:5). I like to imagine being at a table, right there where the devil can see me, and asking God, "Can you please pass me the authority..." or peace or power or whatever I need.

When I was raising my boys and the devil kept lying to me, I learned to pray with authority. In the same way that Jesus said, "It is written!" to the devil when He was being tempted, I had to take dominion over the words of the enemy by using the power of God's Word.

What does that look like? Well, whenever he told me lies about my sons, I'd declare out loud, "Devil! Have you ever read Psalms 100:5? 'The Lord is good. His loving kindness and faithfulness endure to all generations.' My sons will grow up to be 'men of God!'"

When we quote God's Word, the enemy will leave us alone. James 4:7 says, "Resist the devil and he will flee from you." All of us have this authority to take dominion over our minds! It's a personal decision to use that authority—no one else can do it for us and we cannot do it for anyone else.

So, the next time the devil speaks lies to you about God's love or acceptance, remind him of Romans 8:1, "There is now no condemnation for those that are in

Christ Jesus." Repeat God's Word, loudly and with authority, over Satan's attempts to discourage you.

Faith PowerPoint: Like faith, authority is voice activated!

Remember, God does not give us negative thoughts. Any thoughts of failure in your family, finances, or health are not from Him! Learn to recognize the voice of the devil and immediately speak against him. Stop meditating on the devil's lies and start meditating on God's Word instead:

> This Book of the Law shall not depart out of your mouth, but you shall meditate on it day and night, that you may observe and do according to all that is written in it. For then you shall make your way prosperous, and then you shall deal wisely and have good success. (AMPC, Joshua 1:8).

And:

> Finally, believers, whatever is true, whatever is honorable and worthy of respect, whatever is right and confirmed by God's word, whatever is pure and wholesome, whatever is lovely and brings peace, whatever is admirable and of good repute; if there is any excellence, if there is anything worthy of praise, think continually on these things [center your mind on them, and

implant them in your heart] (AMP, Philippians 4:8).

Genesis 1:26 tells us that we are created in God's image, with dominion over the enemy and any other obstacle that would hinder us in our walk with Him! As Jesus said, "Behold I give you power over *all* the power that the enemy possesses!" (Luke 10:19). This dominion is given to us, but most Christians don't understand that it includes finances, relationships, problems, and health issues.

Many times in our business, we'd be faced with an unexpected need, such as an expensive equipment failure. Donald and I would join hands with our administrators and say, "My God will supply all our needs according to His riches!" Then add, "Satan! You will not steal our money! You have no authority over our business, and you have been defeated at the cross of Jesus!" Miraculously, the need would be met from unexpected sources!

I want you to learn to use this God-given authority over financial shortages and in your everyday decisions concerning money. As His Word says, "Thanks be to God who always leads us to triumph!" (2 Corinthians 2:14) and "The Lord will make you the head and not the tail" (Deuteronomy 28:13). Remember—we are created in God's image! In the darkness, He spoke "Light Be." So, what do you need, in accordance with His Word? Speak it!

CHAPTER 7

Raising Our Boys | 65

This dominion isn't just over finances. Every morning as I wake up, I always remind the Lord, "When you died on the cross, you took my sins and my sickness! And by your stripes and wounds I have been healed!" (1 Peter 2:24). It says, "have been," which means it's a done deal!

We need to get a "restraining order" against Satan. Forbid him from entering our thoughts, our families, our finances, and our future plans. I'm a firm believer in rising up on the inside—where the Spirit of God dwells—and speaking out my authority over the devil. God's Word is true, "My God shall supply all my needs according to His riches!" Speak this out loud, then declare to Satan, "You are not going to steal my finances!" And honor God by seeking His kingdom first! (Matthew 6:33)

John 10:10 says "The thief comes only in order to steal and kill and destroy. I came that they may have and enjoy life, and have it in abundance [to the full, till it overflows]" (AMP). So, you can say, "Devil, look! Here's what God's Word says. You read it. I resist your lies and I resist you! You have to run away from me! You dumb devil! Jesus defeated you on the cross! And I am a victor not a victim, I am above you, not beneath. I am the head and not the tail." Speak with authority and quote the Word! Remember, the devil is afraid of you and doesn't like to be reminded of his defeat.

So many of us struggle with thoughts of depression, guilt, temptations, and regrets from the past. The devil will condemn us and try to make us feel guilty and think negative thoughts about ourselves and others. You don't have to put up with that! Rebuke the devil. Tell him to get out of your mind and speak God's Word to him out loud. Personalizing it by adding your name:

"Behold! I give you, [put your name in here], power and authority over all the power the enemy possesses!" (Luke 10:19).

"I, [put your name in here], take every thought and purpose captive to the obedience of Christ" (2 Corinthians 10:5).

Then Jeremiah 29:11, "I, [put your name in here], know the thoughts You have for me—plans to give me a hope and future!"

But, as I've said before, "Easier said than done!" Taking authority doesn't come naturally. When I was about thirty years old and the boys were still pretty young, I was out riding my bicycle around our home and felt something strange happening in my stomach. I hurried to the house and began vomiting up blood. That's never a good thing! It was so bad that I had to keep a bucket by my bed. I hoped it would just go away but, after a day or two, I was getting really scared.

My mother had died of cancer, so of course I couldn't get cancer out of my head. The devil played into my fears. Throughout the night, he'd whisper in my ear, "It *is* cancer. You're going to die of cancer. You're going to die and leave your four sons and your husband all alone." (I don't know why it is, but a lot of women have told me that the devil attacks them in the middle of the night).

Donald was really worried and tried to take the best care of me he could. He called several faith-filled preacher friends, like John Osteen, Kenneth E. Hagin, and T. L. Osborn. They all prayed over the phone for me. He gave me a list of healing Scriptures that I kept reading, but nothing seemed to click in my spirit. I was so frustrated—I believed in healing, so why wasn't I being healed? I laid in that bed for two whole weeks when some verses I'd memorized when I was twelve suddenly rose up in my spirit (that's why it's so important to hide God's Word in our heart!):

> There shall no evil befall you nor any plague or calamity come near your dwelling (Psalm 91:10).
> A thousand may fall at your side and 10,000 at your right hand but it shall not come near you (Psalm 91:7).

Faith began to rise up in my spirit and I declared out loud to myself, "If I am healed, then I will act like it." I raised my hands and said, "Thank you, Jesus, for healing me! If I'm healed, I'll act in faith. No more vomiting blood!" I declared these statements.

So why did those two verses that I'd memorized as a child have more power than all the verses Donald had given me and all the prayers from those men of faith who had successfully prayed for thousands of healings?

Because, as I said, faith and taking authority has to come from our own spirit. No one else can do it for us. It doesn't matter how great their faith is, we have to have faith for ourselves. It was like what happened with the Apostle Paul:

> Now at Lystra a man sat who found it impossible to use his feet, for he was a cripple from birth and had never walked. He was listening to Paul as he talked, and [Paul] gazing intently at him and *observing that he had faith to be healed*, shouted at him, saying, "Stand erect on your feet!" And he leaped up and walked (AMPC, Acts 14:8-10, emphasis added).

As I was saying, I confessed my healing and got out of bed. My legs were shaky because I've been laying down for so long, but I said, "Okay, I'm healed in Jesus's name and I'm not going back to bed. Devil, you get out of my life. I'm not going to give into you." I took authority over his doubts and fears. Remember, this is an authority we all have through Jesus. The devil doesn't have any power over us; all he can do is bluff!

***Faith PowerPoint: Jesus took away all the devil's
authority; now he only has what we give him!***

Not only did I take authority, but I took action. Just like
in Acts 14:10, the lame man's faith didn't do him any
good until he took action and responded to Paul's
command. He put his faith into action and leapt up! I
started walking around the house, taking care of my
boys, accepting my healing, and rejecting the devil's lies.

There are so many more stories I could tell about that
season. We lived there for twenty wonderful and
challenging years, watching our boys grow up, move out,
and get married. It was a little bittersweet when we sold
it and bought a house in Bellevue. We later sold that
house and bought a condo at the top of one of Bellevue's
tallest buildings. The day Donald and I moved into the
condo, the Holy Spirit reminded me of the verse He'd
spoken to us when we left for the Philippines. In Mark
10:29-30, Jesus said, "I assure you and most solemnly say
to you, there is no one who has given up a house or
brothers or sisters or mother or father or children or
farms, for My sake and for the gospel's sake, who will not
receive a hundred times as much now in the present
age..." (AMPC). Donald and I had given $4,500 to God
to be missionaries. Guess how much we sold our second
house for? $450,000. God always keeps His promises!

*So, do I regret making my sons go to church three times
a week and planting God's Word into them? That seed*

brought forth a great harvest, generations serving God and prospering!

CHAPTER 8

Begging Isn't Prayer

───────── ༄ ─────────

As any mother can tell you, we don't stop being a mom once our children grow up and move out of the house. When our youngest son was 33-years-old, he became bitter with people and God and left the church, sending us into a fifteen year storm that was our greatest test of faith. I'll let Paul tell you his own story:

> I was raised in church but was really just going through the motions. Like the seed sown on the rocks (Luke 8:13), I did what I was supposed to on the outside but didn't have any roots. I met my first wife at church, but we left after getting married. She introduced me to drugs and the party life. Drinking, night clubs, and all that. We were divorced within two years.
>
> A couple years later, I got remarried. I knew I needed to go back to church and my new wife said she also wanted to go. We returned to the

church where I'd met my first wife and got involved—singing in choir and other activities. We really enjoyed it and life was great!

We were giving a lot of money to the church and then started having financial troubles. My wife came home one night and said, "I'm leaving you." I was in shock, but honestly kind of glad. Even still, I started praying that she'd come back and Satan wouldn't have my marriage. When it seemed like my prayers had gone unanswered, I started doubting Christianity. Then I began blaming my pastor. Because he owned a Harley, a Mercedes, and a huge house, I accused him of stealing from me. I became very bitter and finally turned away from God and the church. I vowed never to get married again. On Father's Day that year, my dad was praying for dinner and said, "I thank You that all my sons love you." I interrupted him and said, "You can't say that anymore." I was that bitter.

Donald and I prayed every day, desperately begging God over and over again to bring Paul back to Himself and restore him to our family. I just wanted my tenderhearted boy back! But one day, I was reading 1 John 5:14-15:

> And this is the confidence (the assurance, the privilege of boldness) which we have in Him: [we are sure] that if we ask anything (make any request) according to His will (in agreement with His own plan), He listens to and hears us. And if (since) we [positively] know that He listens to us in whatever we ask, we also know [with settled and absolute knowledge] that we have [granted us as our present possessions] the requests made of Him. (AMPC).

Do you see what God's Word says? Confidence...we know for a fact...we know with absolute knowledge...we have what we ask as our present possession! I realized that Donald and I hadn't been praying—we'd been begging! As parents, we'd said, "Stop whining!" more times than I could count, but we'd been whining to God.

That day, we decided to not beg anymore. Instead, we'd thank and praise Him for the answer, even before we saw it! Whenever we heard that Paul was doing something we knew wasn't right, I'd say "Thank you, Jesus, he's coming back. Don't know when... but I think it's about time!" Let's return to Paul's story:

> I continued living in bitterness towards God and the church for fifteen years, then I met Stephanie. I didn't know it at the time, but God was the one who brought her into my life. The pain from two divorces made me struggle with

commitment, but I knew I didn't want to live alone. Besides, she was a committed Christian and clearly had better morals than my first two wives. We began dating, but she had to move to Oregon for a job promotion. Then a job opened up for me at the same office—God was loving and taking care of me! I took the job and moved because I didn't want her to get away. Little did I know that it was all in God's plan. We got married ("He who finds a wife finds what is good and receives favor from the Lord"! Proverbs 18:22) and moved to California a few years later.

After that, I got a job at a wind power company (which was a miracle in itself—God was still loving and taking care of me!). I was laid off, but with six months of compensation, then got a job traveling. It was another miracle—I can see now that God never left me through all of it. I continued traveling for the next two years, then decided to move back to Washington because it was just too hard on Steph to be by herself in a big house with me traveling all the time. She was so lonely without friends or family, but it was all in God's plan!

Around this time, I started thinking more about God and church. The Holy Spirit was tugging at my heart. My job dried up and I was out of work for five weeks, during which time I worried constantly about how we'd make it. I found a short-term job but started drinking heavily after work, knowing I'd soon be out of work again. I was tired of being miserable and not having a future.

It was during this time that Steph told me about a book she'd downloaded, *Heaven Is for Real*. As she talked about it, I just thought, "Yeah, right. Kids have big imaginations." But deep down, I knew it was true. Heaven is real. I started reading and knew I needed to get right with God.

A few days later, working down in Texas, I couldn't fall asleep. I felt God telling me to get down on my knees. I gave in and said, "Oh, okay," out loud, knelt down, and asked the Lord to forgive me and come back into my life. I thought I'd feel something big after that but didn't feel anything special. "Well, that was disappointing," I thought. The next day, I was really depressed—Satan was trying to make me feel embarrassed and want to give up. But I just ignored it all, knowing I didn't want to go back to that same old misery.

When I got back home, I knew I had to ask forgiveness from everyone I'd hurt, starting with Steph. I told her what had happened and asked her to forgive me. Then I went to the rest of the family. I began to read my Bible again, beginning with the New Testament. I started hearing God's voice. The first thing He said to me was, "Be still and know My voice." As I was reading about all the good that God had done for His people, He said, "If I did that for them back then, why wouldn't I do it for you now?"

One day, on a plane ride back home, I was reading the Bible and listening to worship music. I asked God what He wanted me to do and He said, "Keep studying my Word. Your time will come." I was reading about Jesus's parable of the birds of the air (Matthew 6:26). They don't sow or reap or gather but God feeds them and how much more valuable are we? I knew right then I'd never have to worry about anything again!

I started praying for a local job because I didn't want to travel anymore. I posted on Facebook, "My prayer is that others will be saved because of my testimony." The following week, I learned of an opportunity to go with my parents to an annual church convention in the Philippines. Two weeks later, I was at the convention giving my testimony and 20-25 people got saved! And while I was still there, I was offered a job in downtown Seattle and started a few weeks later.

Now I live not only to bring others to salvation but also to let people know they can have a life of happiness, joy, peace, and—most of all—the love of Jesus! Even in tough times I have peace, knowing God will take care of me because He said He would. One day, a man asked for money. I told him I couldn't help but knew someone who could and told him about Jesus. Then I asked if I could pray for him and he said yes. I said a simple prayer for God to take care of his needs, whatever they might be, and told him all he had to do was thank Jesus every day for taking care of his needs. I told him about a good church in Belltown where they would help him.

One last story. Stephanie was complaining to me one day about her job and I started getting really frustrated. What was I supposed to do? So, on my way to work, I said, "Lord, I need Your help with this!" A couple of days later, she was driving and asked the Lord to forgive any sin she may have committed. Right then she got baptized with the Holy Spirit *while she was driving.* God continues to do great things and my story will only continue!

During those fifteen years of praying for Paul and watching him come home, I learned that begging God is not faith. Instead, I discovered that the best way to pray is to declare the Bible verses that support my prayer request—speak it out loud and then believe! This is a totally different way of praying. Most people usually "pray the *problem.*" I've learned to *declare* the answer from the Word. Isaiah 43:26 says, "Put me in remembrance of my covenant." God loves it when we remind Him of His promises!

Faith PowerPoint: Don't pray your problem, pray the answer from God's Word!

Pastor Wendell Smith, in his book *Great Faith*, says, "Quit speaking to God and telling Him how big your mountain is! <u>Start speaking to your mountain and telling it how big your God is!</u>" In the story of David and Goliath, I believe we have a great example of faith and speaking to an obstacle (1 Samuel 17:32-49). David said, "The Lord who delivered me out of the paw of the bear, will deliver me from Goliath."

- He declared God's power (Verse 37).
- He refused to depend on the natural (Verse 40).
- He spoke what God would do through him (Verse 46).

- He did not use human, earthly weapons to defeat the enemy (Verse 49).
- The enemy fled when they saw the power of God (Verse 51).

Romans 4:17-21 says Abraham refused to look at his present circumstances—his impotent body and Sarah being 90 years old. He grew strong in faith as he gave praise and glory to God, who had promised him a child. Then, in verse 21, it says he was fully satisfied and assured that God was able and mighty to keep His Word and to do what He had promised—that's one of the greatest faith verses in God's Word!

Remember, we have the same DNA as Romans 4:17. God speaks of non-existent things as though they already existed. If we could only fully realize this! I have to keep reminding myself that I can speak of non-existent things as if they already existed. What I mean is that you can speak of good health even when you're feeling sick. You can speak of prosperity even when you are in lack. Pray the answer, not the problem, and quote the Word in your prayers. God honors faith. Again, prayer isn't begging and whining, but believing and receiving. It is praising Him for non-existent things as though they already exist.

Faith PowerPoint: Begging and whining are the language of unbelief but praise is the language of faith!

God inhabits praise! Faith is thanking Him before we see the answer and refusing to look at the obstacles or listen to negative conversations. Romans 4:16 reminds us that inheriting the promise is the outcome of faith; it depends entirely on faith. Simply believe God's Word is truth and it will come as He promised.

Prayer is also a kind of praise. I'm telling God how good He is, how He protects me from disappointment and discouragement. He is going to do more than I could ever imagine:

> Now to Him who is able to [carry out His purpose and] do superabundantly more than all that we dare ask or think [infinitely beyond our greatest prayers, hopes, or dreams], according to His power that is at work within us, to Him be the glory in the church and in Christ Jesus throughout all generations forever and ever. Amen (AMP, Ephesians 3:20-21).

That is a great encouraging Word! Since we have this Word from God about what our prayers can accomplish, we can pray with authority and gratefully demand what belongs to us! We don't settle for second best—we declare what is ours in Him whom we serve and have our being (Acts 17:28).

Not only is prayer a type of praise but praise is part of prayer. How? In 1 Samuel 30:6, David was going through a tough time in his life. But it says, "he encouraged himself in the Lord." How did he encourage himself? I believe he began to recount all the victories! Remember Goliath? A very intimidating circumstance! We've all been there. But David declared God's will in the situation! "Who is this uncircumcised Philistine to defy the armies of my living God?" (1 Samuel 17:26).

In that same way, we can ask, "Who is this devil, enemy of the cross that wants to defeat me? He was conquered when Jesus died on the cross!" Remember, circumcision was a sign of the covenant that the Israelites had with God. That's why David called the Philistines "uncircumcised." They didn't have a covenant with God. Covenant is God saying, "If you will give me all you have, I'll give you all I have!" We are now living under the New Covenant—Jesus died on the cross and took our sin, guilt, and shame. By His wounds we were healed (1 Peter2:24)!

I've learned this secret over my years of ministry. People may have a hard time with this, but I think it's so important: Answered prayer depends on *us*, not God. What I mean is that God is, of course, the one who answers prayer, but it's up to us to pray "the Bible way!" Have we declared God's Word and His will for the situation we are praying about?

"If you remain in Me and My words remain in you [that is, if we are vitally united and My message lives in your heart], ask whatever you wish and it will be done for you" (AMP, John 15:7).

"If you ask Me anything in My name [as My representative], I will do it" (AMP, John 14:14). "In that day you will not [need to] ask Me about anything. I assure you and most solemnly say to you, whatever you ask the Father in My name [as My representative], He will give you" (AMP, John 16:23).

Something that makes prayer wonderful is that it allows us to "touch Jesus" in our own special way, just like the woman in Mark 5:25-34. The crowd was pushing and shoving all around Jesus, but she didn't care about the way they were touching Him! What I mean is that in our journey, it's very easy to imitate how others touch Jesus. But she didn't pay attention to them—nor should we. She knew that when she touched Him, she'd be completely healed of her sickness. That gave her the determination to push through many obstacles, not being discouraged by the crowd nor deterred by those who pushed her aside. She just kept repeating, "When I touch Him, I'll be whole." If we could just catch that!

Faith makes all the difference in prayer. Believe in your heart, speak with your mouth (Mark 5:28), and know that He will answer. Think again about how many others were touching Jesus but not being healed. Jesus knew the touch of faith! Pray with determination, like Jacob: "I won't leave here until you bless me" (Genesis 32:26). God loves that determination and godly stubbornness in our prayer.

In that same way, we can find Scripture that supports our prayer, then point to the Word and declare, "This is what Your Word says! So I expect an answer!" Faith hopes for, asks for, and expects! Isaiah 40:31 says it well:

> But those who wait for the Lord [who expect, look for, and hope in Him] will gain new strength and renew their power;
> They will lift up their wings [and rise up close to God] like eagles [rising toward the sun];
> They will run and not become weary, they will walk and not grow tired (AMP, Isaiah 40:31).

Praying with faith determines the answer to our prayers. But Jesus added another very important condition. We can speak to our mountain, as it says in Mark 11:23-24, and receive what we say—what a promise of using our faith prayer!—but don't miss verse 25:

> "And whenever you stand praying, if you have anything against anyone, forgive him and let it drop (leave it, let it go), in order that your Father Who is in heaven may also forgive you

your [own] failings and shortcomings and let them drop. (AMP, Mark 11:25).

It doesn't matter if we've been hurt, misunderstood, or slandered; we must keep our minds, lives, and thoughts clear of any unforgiveness. Nursing hurt feelings are a guarantee that our prayers won't be answered!

I want to let Paul tell the end of his story:

> After I returned to God and apologized to my family, I knew I still had to apologize to my old pastor. He wasn't even aware that I'd slandered him, but I had to do it for my own sake. I went up to him after service and asked for forgiveness. He said, "Yeah, of course!" then prayed with me. Then I felt truly free; I'd done everything I needed to do and there was no more bitterness.
>
> To wrap it all up, Steph and I are still doing great all these years later. She continues to help me grow, especially when it comes to giving. She loves to give. On top of everything else, God has restored what was lost from all the years I walked away. He has blessed us financially—I'm no longer miserable and know I have a great future!

Even with all the storms that we've had to go through, this was a great, rewarding season of my life.

Today, we get together as a family with daughters-in-law and grandchildren and laugh and joke and enjoy each other's company. There is no arguing, no jealousy, and all of them love their mother and father.

So, do I regret everything I had to go through to learn those "prayer lessons"? I wouldn't have learned it any other way. Nothing is lost in God's economy! There is truly a miracle in our mouth.

CHAPTER 9

Generosity or Greed?

———— ༄ঠ৬ ————

From the beginning, Donald and I believed in being generous. Even when we were living on a tiny pastor's salary. We'd give five dollars here to someone and maybe twenty there. But when Donald heard the call to the Philippines, it was a whole new step! We had to sell and give away everything we owned to pay our way. As I said earlier, the denomination we grew up in taught that you couldn't have money and be close to Jesus. "Blessed are the poor" (Luke 6:20), "God has the poor in this world to be rich in faith" (James 2:5), and "You cannot serve God and mammon" (Matthew 6:24). Oh, we knew all those verses!

After we returned home and T. L. Osborn told Donald to use the business to plant more churches; God had to help us think differently about money. One of the key things we learned was that mammon, in Matthew 6:24, doesn't mean money. According to Dr. Derek

Prince, "mammon is an evil, spiritual power that enslaves men and women through the medium of money." _Money_ is a blessing that God gives us so we can bless others, But the love of money, _mammon,_ is a curse.

Donald wrote a book, _Millionaire in the Pew_, several years ago and in it he shared a powerful principle:

> To be trusted with God's wealth, we must determine whether our desire for wealth is to advance the kingdom of God or simply to amass more "stuff." To serve mammon for material gain is the work of an evil spiritual power that grips and enslaves people through their lust for money, and it is never satisfied. It is very difficult for greed to destroy the person who tithes and gives generously to God's work.

This was a brand-new revelation of God's reason for prospering us—so we can give more away! Generosity is one way that we fulfill Mark 16:15: "Go into all the world and proclaim the good news to every creature!" We can't, as individuals, all go into the world. But we can support those who do and then we'll share in the reward for the souls that are saved. We helped many missionaries settle in countries around the world, including Mexico, Philippines, Indonesia, and throughout Africa. I will let Bonnie Deuschle, one of the missionaries to Zimbabwe, tell her own story:

As a young couple called to ministry in Zimbabwe, my husband and I faced many cultural, spiritual, and financial challenges. We started in 1982 with six people in our lounge. And although we had great success in ministering the Word and worship, we battled with lack of resources, skill, and experience. As we persevered in a Third World country, we prayed and cried out for God to intervene and help us. Then, in 1986, we met Don Ostrom. Don was in Zimbabwe for some business ministry meetings and came across our church newspaper advertisement. After inviting us to lunch, we truly connected.

Don and Marlene became our very special friends from that time on. The Ostrom's mentored, encouraged, and financially supported us. They, too, had the experience and understanding of what it was to live on a mission field, sacrificing friends, family and the abundance of the American culture.

They supported our 3,000 seat church building project—a 14 year journey—and came for the dedication service. Marlene suggested we change the name of our church from "Hear the Word" to something catchy like, "Celebration." To this day, Celebration Church (and

Celebration Ministries) stand as a testimony of God's faithfulness and provision.

We now have over 150 churches and 30,000 members, thanks to people like the Ostrom's. Don & Marlene didn't realize it, but we were nearing the point of leaving the country and our ministry when we met them; their generous financial support and blessing made all the difference. To this day, Marlene continues in the legacy of faith, encouragement, hope, and (above all) generosity. We will forever be grateful to the Ostrom's.

Being prospered by God is what allowed Donald and I to be so generous to Bonnie and many other missionaries. What would have happened to Celebration Church if we still believed that you couldn't have money and love Jesus?

One of my favorite verses on generosity is 2 Corinthians 9:7-11: "God loves a joyful, prompt-to-do-it giver whose heart is in the giving." Then in verse 10, "God who provides the seed for sowing will provide and multiply the resources for sowing!" And in verse 11, "We will be enriched in all things and in every way so that we can be generous!"

There are so many ways to be cheerful, joyous, generous people! Acts of generosity does not only apply to big gestures such as giving to missions and to charities. Even a small gesture like providing a meal ticket or helping to fill up a fuel tank can do wonders. How about paying for someone's food at the grocery store, just to bless them? So many ways to bless others with generosity!

I've already talked about how we used our money to do God's work, but we could now be generous on a much bigger scale than a five or twenty-dollar bill. We loved being able to give new cars to pastors in the area. It was so much fun to hand a set of keys to a pastor and say, "It's all yours. Enjoy!" The look of disbelief on the recipient's faces made us even more determined to bless more pastors. One pastor was so embarrassed to drive the new fancy car we'd given him that he parked it behind the church, lest his congregation think he'd used the offering.

That reminds me of an especially fun act of generosity. When our pastor's son, Judah Smith, was only thirteen, Donald shook his hand and left $100 in his palm! Judah never forgot that handshake. And he's now our head pastor! But you don't have to wait until you can give $100—begin with a smaller show of generosity. Just start where you can! It's the spirit of generosity that counts.

Faith PowerPoint: Generosity isn't a dollar amount—just start giving what you can!

As Donald and I gave to His work and were generous in countless other ways, we discovered for ourselves that God always responds to a generous spirit. As Jesus taught in Luke 6:38 "Give! And gifts will be given you, pressed down, shaken, and running over, will men give to you!" We learned that giving to God activates miracles already planned for us!

I realize that sometimes we're embarrassed by God prospering us. It's easy to compare ourselves with others and try to avoid looking prosperous. But instead, let our prosperity be a testimony to His Word. One day, we drove past the Rolls Royce car lot in Bellevue. Donald said, "Wow! I want one of those!" So, we drove home a two-tone gold Rolls Royce. We would get the thumbs down from the Christian community but thumbs up from everyone else! The Christians didn't know how many new cars we'd given away, so we didn't feel guilty for driving one of the most expensive automobiles at that time. We even put "BLEST" on the license plate! It was a real testimony to how God blesses the generous. The more we give, the more we receive. So instead of being embarrassed by God's blessings, just answer, "God keeps His Word!" You aren't bragging but giving testimony to God's faithfulness.

By the way: Never forget that your generosity (or lack of it) is an example to your family. I learned generosity from my dad. He showed me it was very rewarding to give. I watched as he gave to pastors. Sometimes food but always dollars, sometimes even buying a house for the pastor to live in. Then I watched the beds in our nursing homes fill up as other owners were complaining about empty beds in theirs. My dad would often say, "You can't out give God." So true!

Generosity isn't always easy. Financial obstacles will always tempt us to give up when God's Word says to give out! But generosity looks beyond our present circumstances. When we give out of our need—in faith—it opens up pathways for God to show Himself strong on our behalf. Remember, we plant seeds into God's kingdom. Don't measure the harvest by the size of the seed. The seed has potential to grow, multiply, and bring a great harvest: financial, spiritual, and physical!

Faith PowerPoint: Generosity is an act of faith that looks beyond present circumstances.

But even as God prospers us, we can't ever forget about the danger of greed. As Psalm 62:10 says, "...if riches increase, set not your heart on them." Greed will sneak into our lives like an armed robber to steal, kill, and destroy (John 10:10). We must be on constant watch for greed trying to sneak into our hearts—"Guard your heart with all vigilance and above all that you guard for out of it flows the issues of life" (Proverbs 4:23). Another important warning is found in 1 Timothy 6:9:

> But those who crave to be rich fall into temptation and a snare and into many foolish (useless, godless) and hurtful desires that plunge men into ruin and destruction and miserable perishing (AMPC).

Donald and I learned how easily greed can slip in if we don't guard our heart vigilantly. In the early 90's, we bought a condo in Hawaii. It was nice having that condo to enjoy and let other people use. Then we bought three more in Hawaii and two in Seattle.

One day, Donald said, "Well, maybe we should build a condominium building, like on a golf course. We could really prosper that way." Condos were really big business in those days and we were sure we could make a lot of money.

That was when greed started to set in. God hadn't called us to do it; we were doing it for the wrong reasons. Just because we could run nursing homes really well didn't mean we knew how to build a condominium. We didn't realize how much everything would cost and were quickly in over our heads. We had to sell it at a loss to keep from losing more—a half a million dollar lesson!

Donald and I realized that we'd let greed slip in and repented. We committed to staying with the business that God called us to and not letting greed take over. Canterbury Estates is still there on Juanita Golf Course, but the $500,000 is missing from our bank account! Some lessons are expensive, but we never forget them.

Do I regret living a life of generosity? Would anyone regret being so abundantly blessed as to prosper the next generation? Or regret the hundreds of thousands of people attending churches we helped build around the world? No regrets! The reward will be seen in Heaven with countless new believers from many nations.

CHAPTER 10

Breakthrough Faith

∂ ͼ ∂ ͼ

Not long after taking over the business, Donald earned his pilot's license and enjoyed flying our little single-engine Cessna. One day, God told him to buy a twin-engine plane that could carry more people. It cost way more than we could afford but he knew it was God's will. Long story short, God provided and for eight years we used that plane constantly. It saved us a lot of time and money on business trips and we were even able to use it for ministry.

One Sunday, we were at church when an appeal came to help build churches in Liberia. Of course, I knew we'd help, but we also were facing several challenges in our business at the time. We had too many empty beds and were trying to sell a huge, empty ex-hospital that realtors said was unsellable. But Donald leaned over and whispered in my ear, "I believe God is asking me to give our plane to finance more churches in Liberia."

"Give it away?" I said. I wanted to add, "Get thee behind me, devil"! But I knew my husband would never give away his most prized earthly possession unless God had really asked him to do it. We obeyed and let the church know we were donating the twin engine plane for Liberia.

Shortly after this, miracles started taking place. We sold the unsellable hospital, empty beds filled up, and the state increased Medicare and Medicaid payments for residents. Never underestimate the results of obedience! There is a miracle waiting after we obey and give up what God asks us to give.

This is what I mean by breakthrough faith: A special step of faith that opens up more doors. It's like saying, "Okay Lord, this is a big step for us, but it shows we believe You, that we trust Your Word, that we believe You will give us answers in these other situations." Breakthrough faith is doing something big so that other miracles can happen.

Faith PowerPoint: Big steps of faith grow into even bigger miracles!

But breakthrough faith isn't just for people who can give away an airplane! It looks different for each of us. I believe it starts with our mouth. As I said in Chapter 8, we have the DNA of our Father God (Romans 4:17). That means that we can speak of non-existent things as though they already existed. I believe we should declare these "I am" statements:

- I AM an overcomer.
- I AM anointed.
- I AM God's own handiwork.
- I AM healthy.

That reminds me about Donald's favorite declaration: "I am happy, healthy, wealthy and wise!" Here is another great declaration, straight from God's Word: "I can do all things [which He has called me to do] through Him who strengthens and empowers me [to fulfill His purpose—I am self-sufficient in Christ's sufficiency; I am ready for anything and equal to anything through Him who infuses me with inner strength and confident peace]" (AMP, Philippians 4:13).

When we meditate on our problems or unfavorable circumstances, instead of God's Word, it blocks our faith and blinds us to the breakthrough that can happen. As the Apostle Paul said, "So we fix our eyes not on what is seen, but on what is unseen, since what is seen is temporary, but what is unseen is eternal" (NIV, 2 Corinthians 4:18).

Repeating God's Word in our circumstances will bring a breakthrough. The Word becomes a Rhema—God's Word especially applied to your situation—which then becomes a weapon of the Spirit. This is how we take authority over "the enemy of our progress." As it says in

Luke 10:19: "Behold! I give you [put your name in here] power and authority over all the power the enemy possesses." We might not win every battle, but we will win the war! Our weapons are not carnal—guns or swords—but wisdom, and that is better than any weapon of war! As Ecclesiastes 9:17 says, "The words of wise men heard in quietness are better than the shouting of one who rules among fools" (AMP).

So, breakthrough faith begins with a confession from our mouth, but then the Holy Spirit will nudge us and let us know what is holding us back from a breakthrough in our finances or walk with God. We have to be willing to listen and to change so we can "prosper in all things and be in good health, even as our soul prospers" (3 John 2).

In Luke 5:1-8 and John 21:6 we have the example of a breakthrough. Peter and the disciples had been fishing all night, the same way they'd always done it. Then Jesus said, "Cast your net on the other side!" The disciples said, "What? We've never done it that way before!" But Peter listened to Jesus's word telling them to break from their routine. They obeyed and got a breakthrough of a great harvest!

What I'm saying is that it's easy to just live life, going along, and doing certain things, even good things. They may even be acts of faith, but they've become routine. When you want a breakthrough, you have to do something different, something bigger. If you need a breakthrough, it's time to ask yourselves, and God,

"What do I need to release for a breakthrough in my life and finances?"

In financial shortage, the best action is to give an offering. That's faith in God, faith that is an action and takes effort. And don't forget that faith is voice activated! When Jesus spoke to the fig tree in Mark 11:12-14, He told it to die. When the disciples and Jesus came back the next day it was dead. They were surprised, but Jesus said to them, "Have the God-kind of faith constantly!" And what kind of faith is that? Speaking and believing that what we say will come to pass! Romans 12:3 tells us we've been given a measure of faith, the same faith that created the world. Our faith grows as we read, speak, and act on God's Word.

Do I regret giving a major donation to gain a real breakthrough in business? I will never regret being obedient, no matter the cost! The results of big faith far outweigh the temporary sacrifice.

CHAPTER 11

Saying Goodbye

⁀ꙮꙮꙮ⁀

As our business prospered, Donald and I entered a new season of traveling to Africa, England, Indonesia, and almost 40 different countries even as we continued to run our business. As I said earlier, being able to trust God and our facility administrators allowed us to, "Go into all the world and preach the gospel to every creature" (Mark 16:15).

It was a wonderful season but challenging. I had to raise four active boys and make sure they were taken care of. At the same time, I'd determined that my husband wouldn't travel the world without me! I'd seen too many husbands travel to foreign countries without their wives, allowing for all sorts of temptations and causing many problems. In this season, it would always be Donald and Marlene. I was called to make him my first priority!

This commitment made a *big* impact in Africa. My husband spoke to thousands of people in various cities and countries. He would always say "I want the most beautiful gal in the world to stand up!" (He meant me, of course!) This so impressed the Africans because they tended to look at their wives differently. It helped them view women as equal with men!

Let me add that sometimes a small seed—a sermon, teaching, or example—can change a culture or a theology. We shouldn't hesitate to speak what God's Word teaches. Donald and my relationship was an example of Galatians 3:28:

> There is [now no distinction in regard to salvation] neither Jew nor Greek, there is neither slave nor free, there is neither male nor female; for you [who believe] are all one in Christ Jesus [no one can claim a spiritual superiority] (AMP).

Don't ever be ashamed to declare God's Word in any church, community, city, country, or culture. As the Apostle Paul said in Romans 1:16, "I am not ashamed of the gospel, for it is the power of God for salvation [from His wrath and punishment] to everyone who believes [in Christ as Savior], to the Jew first and also to the Greek" (AMP).

I want to talk a little more about marriage. Many times, I've observed a husband and wife sitting side by side at a seminar or in a church service like two strangers. Donald and I always let each other know that we were aware of the other's presence. Just reaching over and holding the other person's hand or giving a loving pat on the arm establishes a bond between the two of you!

Speaking of touch, Colossians tells us this about love: "Wives, be subject to your husbands [out of respect for their position as protector, and their accountability to God], as is proper *and* fitting in the Lord. Husbands, love your wives [with an affectionate, sympathetic, selfless love that always seeks the best for them] and do not be embittered or resentful toward them [because of the responsibilities of marriage]" (AMP 3:18-19). In my many years of marriage, I noticed that men usually like touch more and women like words more. But find out what your partner likes and use it often!

Satan wants to divide us, but God desires a strong, happy marriage. But that doesn't come automatically; it requires effort, thought, and actions. The Bible is filled with verses admonishing us to love one another. We apply them to our brothers and sisters in the Lord, but how about to our marriage partners? First John 3:18 says, "Let us not love merely in theory or in speech but in deed and truth—in practice and in sincerity."

One day, the Lord gave me a revelation from Mark 6:1-6. Jesus entered the synagogue to teach and the people couldn't listen because they saw Him as the "carpenter's son" and not as who He was—the Son of God. I realized that so much disrespect in marriages is caused by wives not seeing their husbands as "a man of

God." Of course, the man must also see his wife as a "child of God." But, in my opinion, most of the disrespect comes from the wives. This is also where the children pick up disrespect for their father.

But husbands also need to remember 1 Peter 3:7:

> In the same way, you husbands, live with your wives in an understanding way [with great gentleness and tact, and with an intelligent regard for the marriage relationship], as with [a]someone physically weaker, since she is a woman. Show her honor and respect as a fellow heir of the grace of life, so that your prayers will not be hindered or ineffective (AMP).

If you don't treat your wife as a child of God, with love and gentleness, it will block your prayers!

Speaking of prayer, let's look at a powerful aspect of marriage. The Word of God states that if one can chase a thousand, then two can put ten thousand to flight (Deuteronomy 32:30). That gives us the image of a greater power found when a man and his wife are in agreement and in harmony. Jesus reinforces this principle. "Again I say to you, that if two believers on earth agree [that is, are of one mind, in harmony] about anything that they ask [within the will of God], it will be done for them by My Father in heaven" (AMP, Matthew 18:19).This is an important reason to solve our differences and maintain harmony in marriage—the devil doesn't want our prayers answered!

Faith PowerPoint: A happy, unified marriage is a powerful spiritual weapon!

Now I want to talk to singles. I know many singles who think that they're only half of a person and that they must be married to be whole. With that mindset, it's easy to jump into a relationship and then marriage. Don't forget that you "are formed and created for His glory" (Isaiah 43:7) and that "everything God created is good" (1 Timothy 4:4), regardless of whether or not you are married!

It's natural to look for a partner that will solve our problems, make up for our weaknesses, and provide the solutions we lack. But *God* has the answers for all those deficiencies, right in His Word! It's important to find those answers and put them into practice—before bringing a partner into our life. Why? Because deficiencies are magnified in a marriage relationship, not diminished.

Don't waste time while you're waiting for God to bring a spouse! Focus on your own spiritual growth and spend time in the Word. Work on the defects in your personality, seek God's plan for your future, and build qualities that make for a great spiritual partner.

Faith PowerPoint: *Spiritual attraction is much more important than physical!*

One final thing. I've counseled many people that think love means sexual relationships, so they begin that before marriage. Not only is this a bad foundation for a long-lasting relationship, but it can also produce a child that has to be raised—usually by a single parent.

I recently met with a young man who has a son and is now living with this consequence every day. I encouraged him to work on a testimony that would encourage others to learn from his mistake. By using God's Word for his situation and giving a vision for the future, I wanted him to tell others what he would do differently if he could. We can all learn from past mistakes. God will use whatever we release to Him for His glory and purpose!

I had the joy of taking care of my Donald through his final days. He never complained and didn't suffer physically. Even facing death, he was always so happy. Believe it or not, it was the greatest joy of my life to watch over him, serve him, and pray together during this time. It is a season I will never forget!

Losing Donald, however, was the beginning of the hardest season of my life. We'd been married for 60 years, a happy and blessed marriage—traveling the world together, building churches, raising a family, and running a very successful business. It was a season of loneliness and even despair. It was hardest when I got up in the morning. I'd wonder: "Who could help fill my day?" "Who can I communicate with today?" "Where are my friends?" I'd check my calendar, hoping for some appointments, then text my local friends to see if they were available.

You see, I'm a very social person. I love being with people, talking, laughing, and visiting. Most of my married life had been filled with traveling the world, speaking to thousands of people, hosting functions in my home, and entertaining famous speakers. I loved that life! Every day was filled with activities with my husband. Social get togethers, church, FGBMI luncheons, dinners, and just being busy most of the time!

I battled the loneliness by repeating all the Scriptures about Jesus's presence being with me. "I will never leave you or forsake you" (Hebrews 13:5). "I am with you always, even to the end of the world" (Matthew 28:20). The lonely feelings were often accompanied by thoughts of despair: "Why live?", "What's the use?", "Who cares?" How did I respond? By speaking God's Word out loud!

Refute reasoning and lead every thought and purpose away captive into the obedience of Christ! Casting down imaginations and every stronghold that exalts itself (author's paraphrase, 2 Corinthians 10:5).

In the midst of loneliness, the devil will try to attack us with feelings of hopelessness. We must guard against the despair of "What's the use?" That will send us into depression. Despair makes us feel like we're all alone. Even Jesus, when He was on the cross, asked His Father, "Why have you forsaken me?" But He also showed He really cared about us:

> So Jesus, seeing His mother, and the disciple whom He loved (esteemed) standing near, said to His mother, '[Dear] woman, look, [here is] your son!' Then He said to the disciple (John), 'Look! [here is] your mother [protect and provide for her]! From that hour the disciple took her into his own home" (AMP, John 19:26-27).

By the way, this is a good lesson for us: In the midst of our trials, always show concern for other people. That helps get our minds off of our problems. But Jesus knew that all His disciples would be lonely after He left. That's why He promised, "I will go away but I will send a helper, a comforter to have close fellowship with you" (John 16:7). What an encouraging Word!

In that season, I found that the most rewarding way to fill the loneliness was to form a group of friends and get into the Word! I've now been blessed to have four such groups in my home every week. We grow together spiritually and enjoy talking and just being friends.

I'll get back to these groups in the next chapter, but I need to give an important caution: In times of loneliness, we must be on guard against reaching out to the wrong people to fulfill our needs. It's not necessarily that the people are wrong, but we're using them to fill the wrong need. Instead of encouraging each other spiritually, we might use them to fill a need of the flesh or a sensual desire, to give us emotional fulfillment or an affirmation that satisfies our pride. It's both wrong and dangerous to expect people to fill a need that can only be fulfilled by obedience to God's will. Remember, whether in marriage or singleness, people can be frustrating! Instead of helping us, they can end up emptying or discouraging us.

During that season, I saw that a crisis reveals who we are inside. "Watch over your heart with all diligence, for from it flow the springs of life!" (AMP, Proverbs 4:23) Hopelessness comes when we have no expectation for the future. Like Proverbs 29:18 says, "Where there is no vision [no redemptive revelation of God], the people perish" (AMPC). No wonder David said, "Search me [thoroughly], O God, and know my heart; test me and know my anxious thoughts;" (AMP, Psalms 139:23) and Solomon said, "The spirit (conscience) of man is the lamp of the Lord, searching and examining all the innermost parts of his being. (AMP, Proverbs 20:27).

CHAPTER 11

Saying Goodbye | 113

Crises and negative situations can bring our greatest hindrance: fear! Fear is paralyzing. As I write this, COVID-19 has hit the whole world and is causing great panic. So many people live in fear of getting it, but fear and faith do not mix! When we allow fear to rule, it means we don't have faith. But when we walk and talk faith-filled words, it casts out fear. Don't ever doubt that we "fight the good fight of faith" (1 Timothy 6:12).

Our faith fails when we take our eyes off the source of our faith: Jesus! Faith must be focused. Matthew 14:27-31 says the disciples saw Jesus walking on water. So, Peter—spontaneous Peter—said "If it's you, command me to come!" He was actually walking on water, until he looked at his surrounding circumstances. When he took his eyes off Jesus, he began to sink. Peter lost his focus!

The devil will continue to put doubts in our thoughts, telling us all the reasons we should be afraid. God saw that lie coming! Jesus told his disciples, "I give you power over *all* the power the enemy possesses!" (Luke 10:19). We just have to take that power. Never forget that it's when we feel the weakest that His strength and power show themselves to be most effective! (2 Corinthians 12:9). That's why I take control of my thoughts by saying, out loud, "Behold! I give you, Marlene, power over all the power of the enemy! And nothing shall by any means harm you!"

As I struggled against loneliness and despair, I did more than take authority over the devil. I also countered the negative with a positive. I'd say (out loud!), "'I know the thoughts and plans I have for you, Marlene,' says the Lord. 'Thoughts and plans for welfare and peace and not for evil, to give you hope in your final outcome!'" (Jeremiah 29:11). Walking by faith allows us to see the future through God's eyes, and it's always bright! That future will develop as we are obedient to walk every day in His will.

It was during this season of loneliness that I received a prophecy through my daughter-in-law Cindy:

> Marlene Joy, God is saying to you, "I've saved the best for last. Look up, now, and know that I have a bright future for you. Take hold of My strong, capable hand, for you and I are about to embark on a season like no other in your life. A season of great purpose and influence. Be listening keenly to the Spirit as I put people in your path and on your mind. For these divine appointments I have set up, and oh, so many await you. One by one, soul by soul, I will guide you to speak into their lives, bringing light, hope, and wisdom. So be ready, look up now and know this new season is not just an end of something but a fresh beginning! Filled with great purpose. Our work on earth is far from done, my daughter, far from done. So, don't let

your heart be troubled but embrace this new season, for you are never alone. Never. And we have much to do together."

I have no lasting regrets from my marriage of 63 years to Donald. I mean, some regrets naturally come to mind, thinking, "If only I had…." But we learn from past mistakes and that's why I'm writing this book!

CHAPTER 12

A New Beginning

———————⊃❦⊂———————

Many years ago, in January of 1980, God provided me a word through a prophet named Dick Mills. He looked at me and quoted Isaiah 60:1: "Arise from the depression in which circumstances have kept you: rise to a new life! Shine, be radiant with the glory of the Lord: for your light is come and the glory of the Lord is risen upon you!" I didn't understand what that word meant when I first heard it. But when I added it to Cindy's prophecy, I realized that God was calling me to continue ministering His Word without my Donald. I also realized this new season was no surprise to Him.

As promised, God has brought me into a totally new season. I enjoy this one more than any other in my life. He has filled my life with divine appointments. Just living in a 43-story condo has been a mission field in itself. Often, in my lonely times, I would take the elevator down 42 floors to the lobby, looking for opportunities to just give a word of encouragement. One time, I was on the elevator with a man that I'd chatted with before. He showed me that all his hair had fallen out from chemotherapy and said that he had stage four lung cancer. I invited him into my condo and prayed for him, telling him that his Creator God knew how to fix him. Today, he has grown a full head of hair and thanks me for my prayers!

I soon discovered that God had even bigger plans for me in this season. He led me to minister to young people by having groups in my condo. It began with two or three young guys meeting in my living room several times a month. I felt the urge to form a group to meet every Monday evening. I had to see—by faith—excited people, hungry to learn more about God, faith, and relationships. By faith, I had to see a full living room and people taking notes, learning more about God's Word for personal application. So, I obeyed God's urging and invited them to start a group. Now my condo is packed with single young guys, hungry for God's Word and direction in their life! Miracles are happening on Monday nights: life-changing decisions are being made, chains of sin are being broken, and legacies are being formed. This will affect whole families for generations to come.

This season of harvest only grows—there are now four groups meeting in my condo! Single guys, businesspeople, married ladies, and single gals. My living room has become a community for young people—some desperate, some lonely—who just have a heart for God. There is no greater joy than watching their lives change, than seeing them motivated to serve Jesus and receive the Holy Spirit. I had to leave the old season of working with my husband to begin a life with a new purpose, new ministry, and new friends. I miss Donald, but I'm not alone. I often quote Hebrews 13:5, "I will never leave you." So we can boldly say "The Lord is my helper I will not fear!" God's Word remains a great comfort.

In this season of hosting groups in my home, I have the challenge of discipling attendees that want to grow deeper in their walk with God. The first principle I teach is from Mark 11:23-24. I tell them, "We must be careful what we say with our mouths. We have what we say! Let's speak what we want, *not* what we have." This principle will change your life!

Proverbs 18:21 says, "Death and life are in the power of the tongue, and they who indulge in it shall eat the fruit of it [for death or life]" (AMPC). According to a top Korean neurosurgeon, the speech center in the brain rules over all the other nerves—the things we speak literally affect the rest of the body.[1] I tell my groups to be careful about speaking negative words. Don't say, "I can't," "I'm too old," or "I'm too young." Always see

---

[1] Paul Yonggi Cho, *The Fourth Dimension* (Plainfield, NJ: Logos Int'l., 1979), p. 67ff.

increase, always see yourselves as capable and more than a conqueror! (Romans 8:37)

Faith PowerPoint: *What we confess, we possess!*

I also talk to them about Luke 10:19 and Ephesians 5:4. We must watch our conversations, our joking, our "small talk," the advice we give, and our discussions with others. As 1 Corinthians 10:23 says, "All things are legitimate, but not all things are constructive." This reminds us to avoid gossip and unproductive speech. Another reminder is in Psalms 141:3: "Set a guard over my mouth." And Proverbs 21:23: "He who guards his mouth and tongue keeps himself from troubles."

I warn them against comparisons. That's a real joy-destroyer—comparing ourselves with someone we think prettier, more successful, more spiritual, or more talented than we are. As 2 Corinthians 10:12 says, "When we compare, measure ourselves with one another, we are without understanding and behave unwisely." We are all made differently, "created in our mother's womb as if embroidered with various colors" (AMP, Psalm 139:15). Let's just be who God created us to be! The enemy wants to divide us, to destroy friendships and peace. But realizing our uniqueness gives us the confidence to overcome comparisons. You are so rare that no one else, in all the billions of people, has your fingerprints! I tell them to be confident, secure, and content with their own personality!

I've also gained so much from them. They encourage me as they learn and grow. One of the young men, Kellen Gildersleeve, told me that when anxious thoughts come to his mind, he closes his eyes and speaks out what Jesus did for him, that He "took those negative feelings on the cross." Then he repeats—out loud—Jesus's qualities and what He would do in that situation. Works every time!

There is so much more to be said, (in fact I'm already working on my next book, which will talk about everything God has done up on the 42nd floor of my building), but here are the characteristics of a true disciple that I share with my groups:

1. A real hunger for God's Word. That means reading the Bible daily!
2. Willingness to surrender anything in our life that doesn't please God.
3. Eagerness to share our testimony with other people.
4. Excitement to see our friends give their lives to serve our God.
5. Faith to *act* on God's Word.
6. Faithfulness to a local church and fellowship with other Christians.
7. Obedience to God's Word in tithing, giving, and helping the poor.

I want to end my book with an encouragement to be obedient to God in everything. Hearing the word "obedience" can bring condemnation but obeying God can be the most rewarding thing we do. As Psalm 40:6 says, "Sacrifice and offering You do not desire but You have given me the capacity to hear and obey." Looking back, I can reflect on the results of my being obedient to God's direction and prompting in my life. The groups now meeting in my condo are one example.

Another example, from many years ago, is when Donald and I met with Wendell Smith, a pastor from Portland, Oregon. He felt called to start a church in Bellevue—that's my city! Donald and I strongly felt we were to help in this venture. We obeyed and today ChurcHome (formerly called The City Church) has grown to thousands in weekly attendance at their campuses in two states and around the world via their app. The current pastor, Judah Smith, has written several books and has ministered to famous actors and musicians. Untold numbers of lives have been affected. People have found new life in Jesus. There have been healings and financial miracles. Families have been restored and missionaries have been sent to many nations.

When we struggle to obey God's leading, sometimes it's good to reflect on the results of when we've obeyed, then think about what would've happened if we hadn't. What if Donald and I hadn't help found that new church in Bellevue? How many generations would have been affected?

Or what if Donald and I hadn't obeyed the call to the Philippines or hadn't continued supporting those churches from our business? Today, there are about 1,000 churches that began with the one church we pioneered in Davao City. Perhaps there would be thousands of Filipinos not in Heaven. How many families would still be living in poverty and how many churches would be hurting financially because their congregations were not taught to tithe?

Faith PowerPoint: Obedience to God will bring miracles, not regrets!

I subtitled this book "Wisdom from a Life Without Regrets" because I don't want you to reach the end of your life and look back, with regret, at all the times you didn't step out in great faith and obey God. It is my prayer that, together, we can make faith great again!

APPENDIX

Words & Confessions

⟳᠗᠗ᠷ

In addition to wanting to "make faith great again," I wrote this book to show the value of speaking God's Word in every situation or problem we encounter. As I've said many times: speak it out loud! Repeat it constantly and with authority:

> "…man does not live by bread only, but man lives by every word that proceeds out of the mouth of the Lord" (AMPC, Deuteronomy 8:3).
>
> "Your word have I laid up in my heart, that I might not sin against You" (AMPC, Psalm 119:11).
>
> "Man shall not live and be upheld and sustained by bread alone, but by every word that comes forth from the mouth of God" (AMPC, Matthew 4:4).

"If…My words remain in you and continue to live in your hearts, ask whatever you will, and it shall be done for you" (AMPC, John 15:7).

"But the Word of the Lord endures forever. And this Word is the good news which was preached to you. (AMP, 1 Peter 1:25).

I've also told you the value of speaking His Word out loud *with authority* in everyday situations: sickness, raising children, marriage. Read God's Word out loud and say gleefully, "Devil, did you hear that? Read it for yourself." So much power in the Word of God—never underestimate the spoken Word!

I wanted to give you this outline and these Scriptures for your use:

I.   **Death and Life in the Tongue**: Proverbs 18:2 – "Death and life are in the power of the tongue, and they who indulge in it shall eat the fruit of it [for death or life]" (AMPC).

   a.   *Our words are like seeds*: What kind of a harvest do you want? Galatians 6:7 – "For whatever a man sows, that and that only is what he will reap" (AMPC).

   b.   *Our words affect our health*: Life and death are in the tongue! My good friend, John Osteen, would correct his wife, Dodie, if she talked about pain. He would say, "Don't say that. Say 'I am healed in Jesus name.'" That was great advice for all of us!

c. ***Our words affect our destiny***:

    1. Proverbs 21:23 – He who guards his mouth and his tongue keeps himself from troubles.

    2. Proverbs 16:23 – The mind of the wise instructs his mouth.

    3. Proverbs 13:2 – A good man shall eat good from the fruit of his mouth.

    4. Proverbs 12:18 – The tongue of the wise brings healing.

    5. Proverbs 14:23 – Idle talk leads to poverty.

d. ***Our words affect our business and prosperity***: To succeed in life and business, we must speak God's Word over every circumstance. Always answer a negative statement from other people with the positive word from God—don't let the devil get a foothold in your mind! When Donald and I would build a new facility and people would ask, "How will you fill this when there's a competitor just down the street?" We'd respond with God's Word: "The Lord shall command the blessing upon you in your storehouse and in all that you undertake" and "The Lord will make you to have a surplus of prosperity… And the Lord shall make you the head, and not the tail" (AMPC, Deuteronomy 28:8, 11-13).

    e. ***Our words can leave a virus in other people's lives***: This can be sowing doubts in their minds or speaking words of scarcity, poverty, sickness, inadequacy, or unhealthy relationships.

II.   Guard Your Words: Psalm 39:1 – "[King David, a 'man after God's own heart'] said, 'I will take heed and guard my ways, that I may sin not with my tongue; I will muzzle my mouth as with a bridle while the wicked are before me'" (AMPC).

III.   Fill Your Mouth with God's Word: Isaiah 59:21 says that God will write His law on our hearts and put His words in our mouths. Remember, we have what we say, not just think!

IV.   Powerful Confessions for You to Use

    a. ***Philippians 4:13*** – "I have strength for all things in Christ Who empowers me [I am ready for anything and equal to anything through Him Who infuses inner strength into me; I am self-sufficient in Christ's sufficiency]" (AMPC). What a great confession to speak every morning! Don't declare your feelings; declare what God says.

    b. ***Romans 10:9-10*** – "Because if you acknowledge and confess with your lips that

Jesus is Lord and in your heart believe (adhere to, trust in, and rely on the truth) that God raised Him from the dead, you will be saved" (AMPC). With the heart we believe and with the mouth confession is made! It's so easy to confess what we see in the natural and only talk about the problems:

1. "My kids don't seem to _____."
2. "My husband/wife always puts me down."
3. "My boss doesn't appreciate me."
4. "I just can't seem to overcome _____."

c. **Romans 4:17** – "[God] gives life to the dead and speaks of the nonexistent things that [He has foretold and promised] as if they [already] existed" (AMPC). God speaks of the non-existent things as though they already existed. Confession is saying God's Word for what we want, not what we see.

1. We have that DNA in our spirit—let's speak victory and blessing into every negative circumstance in our life!
2. Confess healing when health issues arise in our bodies. I love to get out of bed in the morning stating "Jesus! When you died on the cross you took my sins and paid for my health!" and

"Devil! You are not going to put sickness on me. I am the HEALED one!"

3. "Confession by itself will get into my belief system 10%. Using imagination brings it up to 55%. Confession, imagination, and emotion will affect our personal belief system 100%." Tracy Boyd

d. **Romans 4:18** – "[For Abraham, human reason for] hope being gone, hoped in faith that he should become the father of many nations, as he had been promised..." (AMPC). So comforting! Refusing to look at natural circumstances, Abraham hoped in faith.

e. **Romans 4:20-21** – "No unbelief or distrust made him waver (doubtingly question) concerning the promise of God, but he grew strong and was empowered by faith as he gave praise and glory to God, fully satisfied and assured that God was able and mighty to keep His word and to do what He had promised" (AMPC).

About Marlene Ostrom

––––––––––––– ༄༅༅ –––––––––––––

Marlene Ostrom is a Christian leader, businesswoman, and author. Working side-by-side with her late husband of sixty years, she led a successful nursing home business that spanned five states and planted over a thousand churches.

Through the years, she worked with many notable Christian leaders such as Wendell Smith, John Bevere, and John Osteen. She continues to mentor the next generations, teaching them to live adventurous lives of tremendous and expectant faith.

Acknowledgements

———— ୭୧୨ ————

Many thanks to Pastor Judah, who has always honored Donald and me and still calls me "Aunt Marlene." Thanks to my friends Drew Davies, Steve Gutzler, Kellen Gildersleeve, John Bevere, Bob Harrison, and Lyle Wells who encouraged me to write this book, and to my young men's group who inspired me in this endeavor.

Thanks to the dear people in Mineral, Washington and Davao City, Philippines who loved and welcomed Donald and me. Thanks to Tom and Bonnie Deuschle for their contribution to this book. Thanks to Josh Kelley and Mike Acker who helped me edit and publish the book that you hold in your hands. Thanks to Mandy Michaels who typed up this book from my scrawled handwriting.

And, finally, thanks to my sons and daughters-in-law.

"I met Marlene the day I gave my life to Jesus and am now so incredibly grateful to call her a mentor and friend. She's played a huge part in my growth, just as she has in everyone's life she touches.

Isaac Newton said, 'If I have seen further, it is by standing on the shoulders of giants.' Marlene has been one of those giants for me as I've gleaned decades of wisdom and knowledge from her. I'm so excited for the readers of this book, knowing they will catch a vision of the faith that Marlene lives by.

Disclaimer: The wisdom in this book WILL change your life!"

- Kellen J. Gildersleeve

"I've known Marlene Ostrom for nearly 35 years—she is as straightforward, direct to the point, and generous as any person I know! Marlene and her late husband Don have impacted the lives of multitudes: by raising up over a thousand pastors under their oversight in the Philippines, by supporting leaders and pastors through their giving, and by sitting on the boards of numerous Christian ministries and institutions. I, for one, am grateful for their untiring and faithful support of me, my family, and our ministry in Africa!

Every principle Marlene has expressed in her book has a lifetime of experience behind it. Don and Marlene Ostrom were not just hearers of the word, but doers! Read between the lines and listen to the story behind the principles Marlene has scribed — there is spiritual gold in these pages for those who want to live by faith!"

Tom Deuschle
Founder, Celebration Ministries International

There's a phrase out there that 'some things are taught... and other things are caught.' When I'm around Marlene, I catch her faith. When you read this book, YOU will catch her faith! There has never been such a time as now to learn how to speak to whatever mountain of a situation or circumstance you are facing, with the power of Gods word, by faith! I've been around Marlene enough times to know that she doesn't just talk about these things. She lives them! Read and mimic closely the way she declares the Word of God in all things! Now... it's time to make YOUR faith, GREAT!!!

Tyson Hawley,
Real Estate investor, California

In 2019 Tom Hanks starred as Mr. Fred Rogers in *A Beautiful Day in the Neighborhood.* In the movie, a journalist asks Fred's wife Joanne, "what is it like to be married to a Saint?"

Her response not only describes Mr. Rogers, but it is telling of Marlene Ostrom as well.

"It's important you don't think of him as a saint. And the reason it's important you don't think of him that way is

then his message is unattainable, what he was aiming for is unattainable." – Joanne Rogers

In her book, Marlene peels back the curtain and reveals her story and the principles behind her success in life. She shows what living like a saint can lead to and how we can follow in her lead.

Mike Acker

Author, Speaker, Coach, and Founder of Advantage Publishing Group